SERIES EDITOR: TONY HOL...

OSPREY AIRCRAFT OF THE

ACES OF JAGDGESCHWADER 3 'UDET'

John Weal

OSPREY
PUBLISHING

Front Cover
When seven-victory *Experte* Hauptmann Hans von Hahn of JG 53 arrived at Colombert in the Pas de Calais on 27 August 1940 to take over command of I./JG 3 from Hauptmann Günther Lützow, he retained two things from his predecessor's tenure of office. Firstly, Lützow's highly individualistic chevron and triangle *Gruppenkommandeur's* markings were applied to von Hahn's Bf 109 (as was his own cockerel's head emblem). Secondly, von Hahn also strongly believed that a *Gruppenkommandeur* should always lead from the front.

Mark Postlethwaite's dramatic cover painting captures both to perfection. It depicts an incident that occurred on 15 September 1940 – now immortalised as 'Battle of Britain Day' – when nine Bf 109s of I./JG 3 were tasked with providing close escort for a formation of He 111 bombers on a raid against London. As usual, Hauptmann von Hahn flew at the head of his Messerschmitts, and he later described the action in his diary;

'We saw the bombs going down on the target close to the large bend in the Thames. Suddenly there was a yell over the R/T – "Spitfires from right and left!" The show was about to start! With Oberleutnant Sprenger and his 1. *Staffel*, I tucked in close behind the six leading Heinkels.

'I spotted a gaggle of Tommies. On this occasion, for some reason, they didn't dive down on us from above, firing wildly as they raced through our formation, but seemed instead to be intent on burbling in towards us from below left. They approached in line astern, and while still a long way beneath us pointed their noses upwards and sprayed fire from their eight hoses all over the place in our general direction. Then they tipped over and away, ready to repeat the process. But this time we were ready, and went down after them as they broke away again. They obviously hadn't reckoned with this and weren't watching their tails. I quickly got a *"Spitzmaus"* (sic) centred in my sights and let him have it. The next instant there was a blazing torch in the sky in front of me, which then went spinning down wildly towards the clouds below – number 11!'

In fact, records indicate that the unidentified Spitfire was von Hahn's ninth official victory. After claiming his first seven kills as *Staffelkapitän* of 8./JG 53 (plus a further three unconfirmed), his only other success since assuming command of I./JG 3 had been a Spitfire downed south of London on 5 September 1940 while flying close escort to a formation of Do 17s (*Cover artwork by Mark Postlethwaite*)

First published in Great Britain in 2013 by Osprey Publishing
PO Box 883, Oxford, OX1 9PL, UK
PO Box 3985, New York, NY 10185-3985, USA

E-mail: info@ospreypublishing.com

Osprey Publishing is part of the Osprey Group

© 2013 Osprey Publishing Limited

All rights reserved. Apart from any fair dealing for the purpose of private study, research, criticism or review, as permitted under the Copyright, Design and Patents Act 1988, no part of this publication may be reproduced, stored in a retrieval system, or transmitted in any form or by any means, electronic, electrical, chemical, mechanical, optical, photocopying, recording or otherwise without prior written permission. All enquiries should be addressed to the publisher.

A CIP catalogue record for this book is available from the British Library

ISBN: 978 1 78096 298 6
PDF e-book ISBN: 978 1 78096 299 3
ePub ISBN: 978 1 78096 300 6

Edited by Tony Holmes
Cover Artwork by Mark Postlethwaite
Aircraft Profiles by John Weal
Index by Fionbar Lyons
Originated by PDQ Digital Media Solutions, UK
Printed in China through Asia Pacific Offset Limited

13 14 15 16 17   10 9 8 7 6 5 4 3 2 1

Osprey Publishing is supporting the Woodland Trust, the UK's leading woodland conservation charity, by funding the dedication of trees.

www.ospreypublishing.com

Title Page Photograph
A mixed *Schwarm* of I./JG 3 machines, made up of aircraft from all three *Staffeln*, patrol over the Channel during the late summer/early autumn of 1940. The *Emil* in the foreground, 'White 1', is believed to be the fighter assigned to Oberleutnant Lothar Keller, the *Staffelkapitän* of 1./JG 3, whose score by mid-September stood at 15

OSPREY AIRCRAFT OF THE ACES 116

ACES OF JAGDGESCHWADER 3 'UDET'

CONTENTS

CHAPTER ONE
A SLOW START 6

CHAPTER TWO
BATTLE OF BRITAIN AND AFTER 13

CHAPTER THREE
BARBAROSSA – AN ABUNDANCE OF ACES 22

CHAPTER FOUR
MEDITERRANEAN INTERLUDE 32

CHAPTER FIVE
GROWING SOVIET RESISTANCE 36

CHAPTER SIX
DEFENCE OF THE REICH 59

CHAPTER SEVEN
NORMANDY BLOODBATH 68

CHAPTER EIGHT
RETREAT AND DEFEAT 72

APPENDICES 85
COLOUR PLATES COMMENTARY 92
INDEX 95

CHAPTER ONE

A SLOW START

One of the minor anomalies of the wartime German Luftwaffe was the fact that its most famous dive-bomber unit, *Stukageschwader* 2 'Immelmann', was named after the man who was arguably World War 1's greatest fighter tactician, whereas it was a fighter unit that bore the name of the man who is considered by many to be the founding father of the Third Reich's dive-bomber arm! The reasons behind this apparent illogicality are of no relevance here. Suffice it simply to say that the origins of the fighter unit in question, *Jagdgeschwader* 3, date back more than five years before the honour title 'Udet' was conferred upon it.

I./JG 232, one of four new *Jagdgruppen* to be activated on 1 April 1936, was initially set up at Bernburg, some 140 kilometres to the southwest of Berlin. In common with all the other fighter units brought into being during the years leading up to the outbreak of World War 2, this original I./JG 232 was to undergo a complex and bewildering succession of redesignations. Within months it had been renumbered to become I./JG 137, and as such it was later divided into two. Two of its *Staffeln* were used to establish the experimental I.(*leichte Jagd*)/*Lehrgeschwader* (I.(J)/LG 2 of the early war years). The remaining *Staffel* was then strengthened to form the nucleus of a 'new' I./JG 137 during the latter half of 1938.

By this time a second *Gruppe*, II./JG 137, had already been activated at Zerbst, just 30 kilometres to the northeast of Bernburg. And on 1 November 1938 the two units were redesignated to become I. and II./JG 231 respectively. They did not retain these identities for long, however. In the final pre-war reshuffle of 1 May 1939, I./JG 231 was incorporated into the new *Zerstörer* arm as I./ZG 2 (albeit still equipped with single-engined Bf 109Ds), while II./JG 231 finally emerged as I./JG 3 – the first (and as yet only) *Gruppe* of *Jagdgeschwader* 3.

During the two Gruppen's six-month existence, a *Geschwaderstab* (HQ Staff) had been formed alongside I./JG 231 at Bernburg. *Stab* JG 231 was commanded by Oberstleutnant Max Ibel, who remained *Kommodore* after the unit's renumbering as JG 3.

On 26 August 1939, just six days prior to Hitler's invasion of Poland, Oberstleutnant Ibel had transferred his *Stab* JG 3 the 90 kilometres eastwards from Bernburg to Brandis. But JG 3 was not intended for service in the coming campaign against Poland. During the opening month of World War 2 the role of Ibel's command (still comprising just I./JG 3) was instead to provide the aerial defence of the industrial region of central Germany to the immediate south of Berlin. In the event, this area saw no daylight

The man in whose honour JG 3 was to be named, Ernst Udet (centre), is seen here in the mid-1930s wearing the uniform of a *Flieger-Vizekommodore* (Lieutenant-Colonel) of the *Deutscher Luftsport-Verband* (German Air Sports Association), complete with World War 1 medal ribbons and with the *Pour la Mérite* around his neck

Posing proudly in front of the pearl-grey and green Bü 133 *Jungmeister* (L2+08) that he flew as a member of LG 2's *Kunstflugstaffel* (Aerobatic squadron), the young Josef Heinzeller was one of a number of LG 2 pilots who subsequently joined JG 3 and rose to become aces

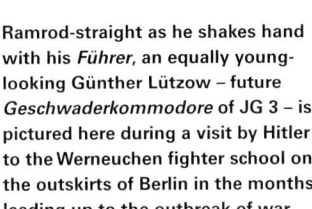

Ramrod-straight as he shakes hand with his *Führer*, an equally young-looking Günther Lützow – future *Geschwaderkommodore* of JG 3 – is pictured here during a visit by Hitler to the Werneuchen fighter school on the outskirts of Berlin in the months leading up to the outbreak of war

bomber incursions of any kind, either from the Polish Air Force in the east, or from Britain and France to the west. By the end of September 1939 *Stab* JG 3 had itself been split into two. Oberstleutnant Ibel took one section to Münster-Handorf, where it became *Stab* JG 27, while Oberstleutnant Carl Vieck – hitherto the *Gruppenkommandeur* of I./JG 2 'Richthofen' – led the other back to Zerbst as the new *Kommodore* of *Stab* JG 3.

Little more than a month later I./JG 3, which by now had joined the *Stab* at Zerbst, also underwent a change of command. The veteran Oberstleutnant Otto-Heinrich von Houwald, who had been *Kommandeur* of the *Gruppe* since its inception as II./JG 137 in the summer of 1938, was appointed to a training post. His place at the head of I./JG 3 was taken by 27-year-old Hauptmann Günther Lützow, an ace of the recent Spanish Civil War.

In early January 1940 Hauptmann Lützow's I./JG 3 was posted to the western front, where it was attached to *Stab* JG 77. For the next four months the *Gruppe* occupied a succession of bases in the Rhineland region, often deployed in individual *Staffel* strength on separate fields some distance apart. This was the period of the 'Phoney War', or *Sitzkrieg*, a fact all too clearly reflected in the unit's as yet pristine war diary, which recorded neither losses nor a single victory.

Meanwhile, back in the heart of the Reich, the operational hiatus that had followed on from the defeat of Poland was being put to good use as the size of the Luftwaffe was rapidly increased. Among the many new units formed during this time were II./JG 3, which was activated under Hauptmann Erich von Selle alongside the *Geschwaderstab* at Zerbst on 1 February 1940, and Hauptmann Walter Kienitz's III./JG 3, established at Jena, near Weimar, exactly one month later. Not surprisingly perhaps, neither of these two *Gruppen* achieved any victories during what remained of the 'Phoney War', although III./JG 3 did suffer the loss of one NCO pilot, whose aircraft crashed in bad weather while on an operational sortie northeast of the Ruhr on 18 April 1940.

CHAPTER ONE

Then, in the early hours of 10 May 1940, the uneasy eight-month stalemate that had existed between the forces occupying the Siegfried and Maginot Lines was suddenly shattered by Hitler unleashing his *Blitzkrieg* against the west. Once again, however, as in the Polish campaign of the previous autumn, *Stab* JG 3 was held in reserve in central Germany as part of the aerial defences of the industrial regions to the south of Berlin. Together with Hauptmann von Selle's II./JG 3, it remained at Zerbst during the opening rounds of the war in the west, awaiting the Allied daylight bombing raids that never came.

During the 'Phoney War' period JG 3 claimed no victories and suffered no combat losses, but there were minor mishaps aplenty, including this one that befell 9. *Staffel's* Oberleutnant Egon Troha. He stood his 'Yellow 3' on its nose while taxiing across Hopsten's sodden surface in mid-April 1940. In Luftwaffe parlance, any machine in this undignified pose was known as a *'Fliegerdenkmal'*, or 'Monument to a flyer'

Things were very different for Oberstleutnant Vieck's two remaining *Gruppen*, both of which had been temporarily assigned to other *Jagdgeschwader*. Having completed its work up at Jena, III./JG 3 had been transferred westwards, first to Detmold and then to Hopsten, little more than 50 kilometres from the Dutch border. Here it was placed under the control of *Stab* JG 26, which was part of *Luftflotte* 2 – the air fleet that was to provide air support for the ground forces' 'feint' offensive through the Low Countries.

Hauptmann Kienitz and his pilots found themselves in the thick of the action from the very outset. On 10 May, the opening day of the *Blitzkrieg* in the west, they claimed four enemy aircraft destroyed without loss to themselves. The first of the four was a Dutch Air Force Fokker D.XXI fighter brought down by 7. *Staffel's* Unteroffizier Matthias Massmann over Rotterdam (this unfortunate Dutchman could thus claim the dubious distinction of being the first of the estimated 6650+ enemy machines that were to fall to pilots of JG 3 during the course of the war).

III./JG 3 would account for a further 42 Allied aircraft before the campaign in the west was finally over, but these victories were fairly evenly distributed between the *Gruppenstab* and all three *Staffeln*. No single pilot managed to take his individual tally to five, although several had achieved the opening kills of what were to grow into impressive personal scoreboards in the months and years ahead. Unfortunately, Matthias Massmann, the unteroffizier who had claimed JG 3's very first success, was not among them. He would be credited with just one more victory – a Spitfire during the Battle of Britain – before he was himself bounced by Spitfires during a subsequent *freie Jagd* sweep over Kent, which resulted in his forced-landing southeast of Tunbridge Wells and spending the rest of the war in captivity.

It should perhaps be pointed out here that the shooting down of five enemy aircraft, which accorded ace status to a fighter pilot in many of the world's major air forces, including the British and American – and which has been used as the benchmark in Osprey's *Aircraft of the Aces* series since its inception in 1994 – was not recognised by the wartime Luftwaffe.

Tucked carefully away from prying eyes in the sky, I./JG 3's fighters await the unleashing of the *Blitzkrieg* against France

Instead, the Germans employed the term *'Experte'* ('expert'), which did not refer to a specific number of personal victories, but was used to describe those fighter pilots of exceptional ability and outstanding prowess.

A pilot's individual score *was* taken into account when it came to the awarding of decorations, but this did not remain constant throughout the war. In the first year of hostilities any pilot credited with 20 victories was almost guaranteed a Knight's Cross, but as the war progressed, and particularly after the invasion of the Soviet Union, this figure was constantly being increased until, eventually, some individuals had amassed scores running into three figures before receiving their Knight's Cross.

While III./JG 3 was operating as part of JG 26 under *Luftflotte* 2 in support of Army Group B's advance across the Low Countries, I./JG 3 had been quietly laying in wait further to the south. Still under the command of *Stab* JG 77, Hauptmann Lützow's three *Staffeln* were dispersed on fields among the Eifel Hills to the east of Bonn. Here they formed part of *Luftflotte* 3, which was to cover the main offensive thrust into France. This was to be launched by Army Group A, which was made up of 44 divisions as against Army Group B's 28 (and included more than twice the number of Panzer divisions fielded by the latter).

After emerging from the wooded byways of the Ardennes, the spearheads of Army Group A were to force a crossing of the one major water barrier in their path, the River Meuse, and then drive headlong for the Channel coast. The success of the German plan depended on the perceived threat posed by Army Group B in the Low Countries, whose advance was intended to lure French and British forces out of their prepared positions in northeast France and up into Belgium. Once the Allies had committed themselves by moving forward, the main assault would be launched in their rear.

It was thus 14 May before I./JG 3 saw its first major action in the west. This was the date on which the French and British first realised where the real danger lay – in the mass of enemy tanks suddenly debouching from the Ardennes to the south. In a desperate attempt to stem this armoured tide, the Allies threw every bomber they could muster against the Meuse bridges around Sedan. During what was to become known in Luftwaffe circles as 'The Day of the Fighters', 89 Allied aircraft were shot down.

I./JG 3 was not directly involved over the Sedan bridgeheads. Its task was to provide low-level aerial cover for German troop movements some 60 kilometres downstream from the main crossing points. This resulted in the *Gruppe* claiming eight enemy fighters without loss. Among the five pilots to be credited with their first victories of the war was *Gruppenkommandeur* Hauptmann Günther Lützow, who downed a brace of French Curtiss H-75s to the northwest of the Belgian town of Dinant.

Further claims followed over the course of the next 48 hours (including a third Curtiss for Hauptmann Lützow), but it was 17 May – the day the *Gruppe* moved forward to Philippeville, close to the Franco-Belgian border – that was to bring I./JG 3 its greatest success of the entire campaign in the west.

At dawn on the 17th, 12 Blenheim IVs of RAF Bomber Command's No 82 Sqn had taken off from their base at Watton, in Norfolk, to attack the German armour pouring through the 'Gembloux gap' – the 45 kilometre-wide plateau between the Rivers Dyle and Meuse that had been the historic invasion route into France for centuries past. The Blenheim IVs were intercepted by six patrolling Bf 109s of 1./JG 3. In a running battle reportedly lasting the best part of an hour, the German fighters claimed every single one of the British bombers shot down (in fact, a solitary badly damaged Blenheim IV had managed to limp back to Watton, where it was promptly declared a write-off).

Later that same afternoon and evening the pilots of 1./JG 3 added two more Blenheim IVs and another five French Curtiss H-75s to their *Staffel* scoreboard. These brought their total number of claims for the day to 19 and, at the same time, provided *Jagdgeschwader* 3 with the first two of the more than 300 five-victory aces that were to serve in its ranks during the course of the war.

Having already been credited with four of the morning's Gembloux Blenheim IVs, Oberfeldwebel Max Bucholz claimed a Curtiss fighter south of St Quentin shortly after midday. This not only took his personal score to five enemy aircraft destroyed, it also made him the first of JG 3's many subsequent 'five-in-one-day' aces.

Seen here (facing camera) during the latter stages of the Battle of Britain, Leutnant Gerhard Sprenger made his first five victory claims against RAF Blenheim IVs over France in May 1940. He would achieve just one more victory – a Spitfire downed southeast of London on 2 September 1940 – before being reported missing (shot down by Hurricanes) on 16 May 1941

The last of the seven kill bars adorning the rudder of Hauptmann Günther Lützow's E-4 is for the French Curtiss H-75 brought down during Operation *Paula* on 3 June 1940. Note that the *Kommandeur's* machine has clearly been oversprayed to give it a dapple finish since his third victory less than three weeks earlier

II./JG 3 produced no aces during the *Blitzkrieg* in the west. *Gruppenkommandeur* Hauptmann Erich von Selle (seated) *had* achieved three victories over France, to which he would add another four during the Battle of Britain. The last of these latter kills was a Hurricane brought down on 29 September 1940 – just 24 hours before he relinquished command to join the newly forming nightfighter arm

It was one of the two Blenheim IVs downed later that afternoon that gave Leutnant Gerhard Sprenger his fifth. All four of Sprenger's previous victims had been Blenheim IVs too, the first claimed over Belgium on 15 May and the others being three of the machines of the Gembloux force.

For the next two weeks I./JG 3 was in almost constant action as the British Expeditionary Force (BEF) was pushed back towards the Channel coast. Two further aces emerged during this period. Oberleutnant Lothar Keller, the *Staffelkapitän* of 1./JG 3, caught a French Morane-Saulnier MS.406 over Cambrai on 21 May – his fifth enemy fighter in eight days – while another pair of MS.406s despatched by Hauptmann Lützow south of Amiens late on 31 May took the *Gruppenkommandeur's* own score to six.

The successful evacuation of the BEF from Dunkirk marked the end of *'Fall Gelb'* ('Case Yellow'), the opening round of the *Blitzkrieg* in the west. Now it was time to launch *'Fall Rot'* ('Case Red'), the second half of the campaign, which was to be directed against the bulk of the French forces to the south and west. *Fall Rot* was prefaced on 3 June 1940 by Operation *Paula* – a concerted air attack on French airfields, aircraft factories and other installations in and around the Greater Paris area. Still operating under JG 77 control, Hauptmann Lützow's I./JG 3 was tasked with escorting a *Geschwader* of Do 17s sent to bomb enemy airfields around Meaux to the northeast of the French capital. Due to a communications breakdown, the raid did not go entirely according to plan and I./JG 3 ended the day with just one victory – a Curtiss H-75 shot down over the forest of Compiègne, which was kill number seven for the *Gruppenkommandeur*.

It was at this late juncture that Oberstleutnant Vieck's *Stab* JG 3 was finally relieved of its tedious and unrewarding homeland defence duties and transferred forward to the fighting front in France. On 4 June the *Stab* touched down at Valheureux, to the west of Arras. And now, for the first time since their activation, all three *Gruppen* of the *Geschwader* were to operate together as a single force.

During *Fall Rot* JG 3's fighters supported the ground

forces pushing west along the Channel coast and down past Paris towards the valley of the Loire. While the *Stab* remained at Valheureux throughout this second stage of the campaign in the west, Vieck's three *Gruppen* had advanced as far as Le Mans by the time of the French surrender. But opposition in the air was disorganised and piecemeal, which in turn meant that neither II. nor III./JG 3 managed to produce an ace during this final phase of the war against France.

The more experienced I. *Gruppe* welcomed one new ace into its ranks, however. Late on the morning of 7 June, 2. *Staffel's* Leutnant Helmut Tiedmann bounced an unsuspecting Fighter Command Hurricane close to the Channel coast to add to the four victories he had already achieved during *Fall Gelb*. And just over 24 hours later Hauptmann Lützow claimed his ninth, and last, enemy aircraft of the campaign by downing a single Blenheim IV near Abbeville. Oberleutnant Lothar Keller had been presented with a unique opportunity to go one better. A pair of Polish-flown Caudron C.714 fighters, having just attacked a formation of Luftwaffe Do 17 bombers north of Dreux, then inadvertently attached themselves to Keller's 1./JG 3! Before the enemy pilots had time to realise their mistake, Keller had shot both of them down. The second of the two Caudrons took the *Staffelkapitän's* personal score to ten, thereby making him the first pilot from JG 3 to reach double figures.

Despite its slow start, the *Geschwader's* collective scoreboard at the end of the *Blitzkrieg* in the west displayed a very creditable 180+ enemy aircraft destroyed (almost exactly half that total having been amassed by Günther Lützow's I. *Gruppe* alone). JG 3 was not the most successful *Jagdgeschwader* of the campaign, but the unit was not at the bottom of the victory table either. Most importantly perhaps, its pilots had grown in experience and confidence. They would need both in abundance for the new challenge that now awaited them on the far side of the English Channel.

Another photograph of Hauptmann Günther Lützow's machine, still bearing seven kill bars, but now displaying an entirely different, and highly unusual, set of *Kommandeur's* markings consisting of a chevron and triangle of equal size placed one behind the other

THE BATTLE OF BRITAIN AND AFTER

Many accounts suggest that the regrouping of the Luftwaffe's forces along the Channel coast after the defeat of France was an unhurried, almost leisurely affair. This may well have been true of some units, but little time seems to have been lost in transferring JG 3 to its new area of operations. Even before the armistice with the French had been signed, Oberstleutnant Carl Vieck's three *Gruppen* had been pulled out of Le Mans and sent back northeastwards to take up residence on fields in the Pas-de-Calais region.

Yet despite its proximity to the Straits of Dover, JG 3 played little part in the opening rounds of what was to become the Battle of Britain. Rather than escorting the Luftwaffe's bombers and Stukas on their first exploratory raids out over the Channel, the *Geschwader* was once again put on a defensive footing, this time guarding the French coast against British bombing raids.

Thus, in the six weeks from late June until mid-August 1940, while the historic battle steadily escalated around them, the pilots of JG 3 were involved in only one action of note. This occurred on the afternoon of 10 July, when six Blenheim IVs of No 107 Sqn took off from Wattisham to attack an airfield near Amiens. After their formation had been broken up by German flak, the British bombers were set upon west of Arras by the Bf 109s of 9./JG 3, who claimed all six shot down – although, as in the earlier Gembloux raid, one of the Blenheim IVs *did*, in fact, manage to make it back to base.

In passing, it should perhaps be mentioned here that the thorny subject of overclaiming runs like a thread throughout much of the literature dealing with the air war of 1939-45. The overwhelming majority of fighter pilots of all nations undoubtedly made their claims in all good faith. But, despite the authorities setting stringent corroborative criteria before allowing a kill – material or photographic evidence, eyewitness reports and the like – overclaiming remained a problem. Given the chaos and confusion of an air battle and the split-second, life-or-death decisions that had to be made, errors were inevitable. And as the war progressed, and those air battles grew both in complexity and in the numbers of aircraft involved, so the mistakes increased.

Even in fairly simple and straightforward actions such as the Blenheim IV raid on Amiens of 10 July 1940, where all six of the attackers were acknowledged at the time as confirmed victories, but where Allied records have since revealed that 'only' five were actually lost, it is now almost impossible to determine which of the six pilots' claims should be disallowed. This is why all listings of Luftwaffe fighter pilots' scores (including, it is freely admitted, the appendices at the end of this work) must be treated with a certain amount of caution. Very few such tables

CHAPTER TWO

The first JG 3 ace to be lost in action, seven-victory Oberleutnant Helmut Tiedmann of 2. *Staffel* pulled off a neat belly-landing in a Kentish cornfield shortly after midday on 18 August 1940 and remained on the run for more than 12 hours before finally being captured in the early hours of the following morning. The hay used as a temporary camouflage until his 'Black 13' can be recovered has failed to hide the red *Tatzelwurm* on the engine cowling and the yellow (?) segment at the top of the rudder that was used to denote the machine of a *Staffelkapitän*

can boast 100 per cent accuracy, but the errors they contain are relatively minor. So, although not always numerically exact, they *do* provide the best possible measure of a pilot's individual performance and standing.

After III./JG 3 had claimed the six Blenheim IVs west of Arras on 10 July, it was another of the same *Gruppe's* pilots who was credited with a solitary (and unidentified) Hurricane northeast of Folkestone four days later. A whole month would then pass – a month that culminated in the fiasco of '*Adlertag*' – without JG 3 scoring a single success.

Indeed, it was not until 14 August that the *Geschwader* claimed its next kill. The Hurricane that went down off Dover on that date was the first for future Knight's Cross winner Leutnant Franz Beyer of 8./JG 3. Twenty-four hours later it was the turn of I. *Gruppe* to open its Battle of Britain scoreboard. This was another Hurricane, which was to provide the *Kapitän* of 2. *Staffel*, Oberleutnant Helmut Tiedmann, with his seventh, and last, victory of the war. Tiedmann was himself forced to land his damaged 'Black 13' near Maidstone, in Kent, after an encounter with RAF fighters just three days later – the first *Jagdgeschwader* 3 ace to be lost in action.

By this time JG 3 had at last been relieved of most of its defence duties along the French Channel coast and was finally beginning to venture over into southern England. This operational change was clearly reflected in the multiple daily scores that the *Geschwader* now started to amass. On 16 August Hauptmann Günther Lützow, the *Kommandeur* of I. *Gruppe*, took his personal tally into double figures with the downing of a Spitfire over Kent. And it was on this same date that II./JG 3 entered the Battle of Britain fray by claiming no fewer than five Spitfires (almost certainly from No 266 Sqn) over the Ashford-Canterbury area. Among the successful pilots were two more future Knight's Cross recipients, Unteroffiziere Alfred Heckmann and Walter Ohlrogge.

On 18 August another two pilots reached their 'fifths' when 2. *Staffel's* Leutnant Hans-Herbert Landry and Oberleutnant Willy Stange, the *Kapitän* of 8. *Staffel*, were each credited with a Hurricane. Forty-eight hours later Leutnant Franz Achleitner of 9./JG 3 also took his score to five by bringing down a Spitfire. Although claimed over the Straits of

Dover, Achleitner's victim was, in all probability, the No 65 Sqn machine that was written-off in a forced-landing after being damaged by a Bf 109 over the Thames Estuary (this being the only Spitfire lost on 20 August).

Despite such individual successes as these, however, the recently elevated *Reichsmarschall* Hermann Göring was far from happy with the performance of his fighters in the battle to date. In an effort to remedy what he saw as their 'lack of aggression', he ordered what was tantamount to a purge among the older *Kommodores* of his *Jagdgeschwader*. Most of these World War 1 veterans were shunted upstairs into staff positions. They were replaced by some of the so-called 'Young Turks' – fighter pilots who had demonstrated their combat skills in the recent *Blitzkrieg* against France. Although their bravery in the air was indisputable, some of these younger officers lacked the necessary maturity to command a large body of men on the ground. But JG 3 was more than fortunate in this respect. Upon the departure of Oberstleutnant Carl Vieck on 21 August, the man who took his place at the head of the *Geschwader* was Hauptmann (later Major) Günther Lützow, the long-serving *Kommandeur* of I. *Gruppe*.

Günther Lützow has been described by an eminent German aviation historian as 'one of the outstanding personalities of the Luftwaffe's fighter arm – the model of a dedicated officer, admired and respected by all'. After serving for very nearly two years in command of JG 3, he would rise to high rank and position within the Jagdwaffe, only to fall foul of Hermann Göring for having the temerity to question the *Reichsmarschall's* mishandling of Germany's fighter forces. An irate Goring responded by accusing Lützow of mutiny and banishing him to what was then the backwater of the Italian theatre. This care and concern for the well-being of his subordinates was typical of Lützow. It had been in evidence from the moment he assumed command of I./JG 3. But 'Franzl' Lützow was no mere armchair warrior – he also led his men from the front.

Beginning with a brace of Defiants (from the hapless No 264 Sqn) shot down off the north Kent coast on 26 August, Günther Lützow was to claim all but one of the nine victories credited to the *Stab* JG 3 during the course of the Battle of Britain. This took his overall score to 18 and, in the process, earned him the *Geschwader's* first Knight's Cross, awarded on 18 September when his tally stood at 15.

Posted in from JG 53 to replace Günther Lützow at the head of I. *Gruppe*, Hauptmann Hans von Hahn has clearly retained his predecessor's unusual *Kommandeur's* markings. Note too the striking personal insignia ('*Hahn*' means 'cockerel' in German, a fact also seized upon by the better known Hans 'Assi' Hahn of JG 2 'Richthofen')

The man brought in to succeed Hauptmann Lützow at the head of I./JG 3 was Hauptmann Hans von Hahn. The first of many existing aces who would join the ranks of the *Geschwader* as the war progressed, von Hahn had been the *Staffelkapitän* of 8./JG 53 since that unit's formation in September 1939. With seven kills already under his belt, Hauptmann von Hahn took over the *Gruppe* just as the battle was entering a new round of bombing raids on the southeast of England.

The object of these raids was to sap Fighter Command's strength by forcing it into the air and into action. As part of the large force of Bf 109s concentrated in the Pas-de-Calais to provide escorts for Göring's bomber formations, JG 3 soon found itself in the thick of the fighting. In the last eight days of August 1940 six of the *Geschwader's* pilots took their personal scores to five and above. But those same eight days also saw two more promising operational careers brought to premature ends when another pair of newly fledged five-victory aces followed 2. *Staffel's* Helmut Tiedmann into British captivity.

The 'one who was to get away'! With four victories, Leutnant Franz von Werra – seen here keeping a wary eye on 'Simba', II./JG 3's lion cub mascot – had been the *Gruppe's* highest scorer of the French campaign. The three kill bars just visible on the tailfin of his machine date this photograph to between 22 May (when he claimed Nos 2 and 3 – a brace of twin-engined Bréguet 690s) and 3 June (his fourth – a Morane-Saulnier MS.406)

III./JG 3 suffered mixed fortunes on 24 August. Two of the four Spitfires claimed by the *Gruppe* over Kent and Essex on that date made aces out of Leutnant Leonhard Göttmann and Unteroffizier Josef Keil, but the action had cost 9. *Staffel* two pilots shot down and captured. One of them was Leutnant Franz Achleitner, who was fished from the waters of the Thames Estuary after parachuting from his damaged 'Yellow 8' off the Kent coast.

On 28 August 7. *Staffel's* Feldwebel Josef Bauer claimed a brace of Spitfires (probably up from Hornchurch) on the Essex side of the estuary to take his score to six. That same day I. *Gruppe's* Leutnant Heinz Schnabel was credited with his fifth kill (a Spitfire over northern Essex), although for I./JG 3 this success was marred by the loss of the *Gruppenstab's* Leutnant Hans-Herbert Landry, who was badly wounded in a clash with RAF fighters over Dover. References differ as to whether Landry bailed out or forced-landed, but records indicate that he died of his wounds a month later.

The day's honours undoubtedly went to II./JG 3, whose *Gruppen-Adjutant*, a certain Oberleutnant Franz von Werra, claimed his fifth victory (a Spitfire, almost certainly from No 603 Sqn) over north Kent, before then bagging a trio of Hurricanes to take his overall score to eight. Just over a week later, on 5 September, Franz von Werra failed to return from another bomber escort mission over Kent, having been brought down west of Staplehurst by No 603 Sqn's Plt Off 'Stapme' Stapleton. Having pulled off a perfect belly-landing and been taken prisoner, von Werra was later transported to Canada. There, he would gain fame as 'the one who got away' by escaping across the border into the then still neutral USA.

By the time he forced-landed in Kent, von Werra had upped that total to eight (the last four being a quartet of RAF fighters all claimed on 28 August 1940). An RAF sergeant inspects the record carefully kept by von Werra on the tailfin of his E-4, which also includes five aircraft destroyed on the ground (downward-pointing arrows)

This well-known photograph of Knight's Cross winners Major Günther Lützow (left) and Hauptmann Wilhelm Balthasar (centre) shows an even more impressive scoreboard which, in close-up . . .

. . . is revealed to be that of Wilhelm Balthasar. It meticulously records every one of the 36 victories that Balthasar achieved during the recent *Blitzkrieg* campaign in the west, both in the air and on the ground (upward- and downward-pointing arrows, respectively). They are in strict chronological order starting at bottom left immediately above the aircraft's *Werk-Nummer*. Note also the top row indicating the five Spitfires claimed by Balthasar since assuming command of III./JG 3 (and already two more than shown in the photograph above). Also apparent in this shot (but not in the previous one) is the fact that, apart from the immediate area of the scoreboard, the machine's rudder is painted yellow

On 31 August Hauptmann Kienitz relinquished command of III./JG 3. Arriving via a brief stint as chief instructor at the Werneuchen-based *Jagdfliegerschule* (fighter pilot school) 1, the officer who replaced him on 1 September was already wearing the Knight's Cross. As the *Staffelkapitän* of 1./JG 1 (the later 7./JG 27), Hauptmann Wilhelm Balthasar had been the Luftwaffe's most successful pilot during the *Blitzkrieg* in the west – he emerged from that campaign with 23 aerial victories to his credit, plus 13 enemy aircraft destroyed on the ground. Balthasar's first victory as *Gruppenkommandeur* of III./JG 3 was a Spitfire (probably from No 66 Sqn) shot down during a fierce dogfight over the Thames Estuary on the morning of 4 September – Balthasar was himself wounded in the engagement.

It was clear that the battle was now approaching its climax. In the first two weeks of September 1940 three more pilots of JG 3 achieved their fifth kills – Leutnants Eberhard Bock and Helmut Meckel, both of I. *Gruppe*, on 2 and 7 September respectively, and II. *Gruppe's* Oberleutnant Erich Woitke on 9 September. Oddly, while Meckel and Woitke were each credited with a Spitfire, Leutnant Bock (the newly appointed *Staffelkapitän* of 3./JG 3) identified the victim he had brought down southeast of London as a French Morane!

On the other side of the coin, the first half of September also witnessed an increased number of casualties. Among them, in addition to the wounding of Wilhelm Balthasar and the forced-landing of Franz von Werra already mentioned, were several more of the *Geschwader's* newly minted aces. On 5 September three pilots from I./JG 3 failed to return from a mission to the London area. One of them was Leutnant Heinz Schnabel of 1. *Staffel*. At almost the same instant as Oberleutnant von Werra was belly-landing at Marden (British records give the time of both incidents as 1010 hrs), but some 30 kilometres to the east at Aldington on the edge of Romney Marsh, 'Hannibal' Schnabel came screaming in for a high speed, wheels-up landing of his own. The impact tore the engine of Schnabel's 'White 6' from its mounts. He himself sustained severe spinal injuries, which meant that he ended up not simply behind British wire, but encased in a plaster cast as well.

Taking the parallel with Franz von Werra one step further, after recovering from his injuries Heinz Schnabel also succeeded in escaping from captivity. Unlike his famous compatriot, however, he just failed to make it home. In prison camp he had teamed up with Oberleutnant Harry Wappler, the only surviving crew member of a Heinkel bomber that had been brought down by hitting a balloon cable while returning from a night raid on Ellesmere Port. After breaking out of camp, the pair had audaciously stolen a Miles Magister trainer, only to have to abandon their plan to fly to the continent when they discovered that they were running dangerously low on fuel while still over East Anglia. Leutnant Schnabel was thus destined to sit out the rest of the war as a prisoner. Given the fact that Franz von Werra was killed after returning to operations with JG 53, it was perhaps 'Hannibal' Schnabel who had had the lucky escape after all!

Leutnant Heinz Schnabel's high-speed belly-landing on 5 September tore the engine of his 'White 6' from its mounts. Although 'Hannibal' Schnabel had been credited with six kills by the time of his enforced arrival in Kent, there are only *two* victory bars visible here at the top of the rudder. The sheep, meanwhile, remain totally oblivious to the history being made all around them

On 7 September, two days after von Werra's and Schnabel's forced-landings, the *Geschwader* experienced the loss of its first ace to be killed in combat when Oberleutnant Leonhard Göttmann of the *Gruppenstab* III./JG 3 was shot down over the Thames Estuary. 7. *Staffel's* Feldwebel Josef Bauer was to suffer a similar fate on 9 September, being declared missing after being seen going down into the Channel during a clash with British fighters. Another pilot of 7./JG 3, Unteroffizier Matthias Massmann, also failed to return to Desvres on this date. He had forced-landed near Hawkhurst, in East Sussex, with a damaged engine. Massmann was not an ace (a Spitfire credited to him on 29 August had had taken his score to just two), but he *had* been responsible for the *Geschwader's* very first kill of the war – that Dutch Fokker D.XXI claimed on the opening day of the *Blitzkrieg* in the west.

Now commemorated annually as Battle of Britain Day, 15 September 1940 saw the emergence of two more JG 3 aces. Both were Feldwebeln serving with III. *Gruppe*. Rudolf Saborowski's fifth was a Hurricane, possibly one of the two machines reported lost by No 229 Sqn over Sevenoaks shortly before midday. But the identity of Hans Stechmann's Spitfire, claimed 20 minutes later in the same area, is harder to establish.

The battle had undoubtedly reached a peak on 15 September, as is illustrated by the fact that JG 3 managed to produce only one more ace during the remainder of the year. Oberleutnant Egon Troha, the *Kapitän* of 9. *Staffel*, was credited with his fifth on 26 October. And in this instance his victim was almos certainly a Hurricane of No 229 Sqn, one of two shot down by Bf 109s while busily attacking a Luftwaffe He 59 air-sea rescue floatplane off the French coast west of Boulogne. Egon Troha was not to enjoy his acedom status for long. Just

9. *Staffel's* Feldwebel Hans Stechmann claimed his fifth kill (a Spitfire) on 15 September 1940. Since that date his score has apparently doubled, for an obliging groundcrewman is seen here adding a tenth victory bar to the rudder of his 'Yellow 3'. There is, however, a slight mystery. This photograph was reportedly taken at Desvres, France, in February 1941, whereas Stechmann was not officially credited with his tenth until 48 hours into *Barbarossa*!

Having got Oberleutnant Egon Troha's 'Yellow 5' back onto its clearly damaged undercarriage, a British army recovery crew prepare to remove the Daimler Benz DB 601A engine. Note III./JG 3's new 'Battleaxe' *Gruppe* badge and the name *Erika* on the starboard side of the cowling lying in the foreground bottom right

The new *Kommandeur* of III. *Gruppe*, Hauptmann Walter Oesau (right), is pictured here leaning on the mount of his predecessor, whose scoreboard is still displaying that top row of five victories (although, oddly, Hauptmann Balthasar was credited with *six* Spitfires during his time in command of III./JG 3)

three days later he was himself bested in a dogfight with another formation of Hurricanes (of No 253 Sqn?) and forced to make an emergency landing northwest of Dover.

The marked reduction in daylight fighter activity during the final quarter of 1940 allowed many of the Channel-based *Jagdgeschwader* to make command changes. On 30 September Hauptmann Erich von Selle, the *Gruppenkommandeur* of II./JG 3, had taken up a staff appointment with the newly forming nightfighter arm. For the best part of the next two months the *Gruppe* was led in an acting capacity by Oberleutnant Erich Woitke, the *Staffelkapitän* of 6./JG 3. It was not until the end of November, when Erich Woitke departed to assume command of II./JG 52, that a permanent replacement for Erich von Selle took office at the head of II./JG 3. This was Oberleutnant (later Hauptmann) Lothar Keller, hitherto the *Staffelkapitän* of 1./JG 3. The elevation of Keller and Woitke to *Gruppenkommandeure* positions led in turn to Oberleutnants Gerhard Sprenger and Heinrich Sannemann being appointed the *Kapitäne* of 1. and 6. *Staffeln*, respectively.

In the meantime, Hauptmann Wilhelm Balthasar, the *Gruppenkommandeur* of III./JG 3, had recovered from his wounds of 4 September and returned to operations. He had claimed a brace of Spitfires on each of three separate days between 23 September and 29 October. These had taken his personal total to 29. He had then relinquished command of III. *Gruppe*, reportedly for a further period of rest and recuperation, before being appointed *Kommodore* of JG 2 'Richthofen' in early 1941. The man who had been brought in on 11 November 1940 to lead III./JG 3 in Balthasar's stead was another veteran of the Condor Legion. Hauptmann Walter Oesau had scored eight victories in Spain against Balthasar's seven. Since the start of the war he had amassed a further 39 kills with III./JG 51 – latterly as that unit's *Gruppenkommandeur* – and, like Balthasar, he too arrived at III./JG 3 already sporting the Knight's Cross.

As the second winter of the war closed in, daylight operations came almost to a standstill. For more than six weeks JG 3 did not file a single claim for an enemy aircraft destroyed, but the locations given for the *Geschwader's* final successes of 1940 and its first of 1941 are most illuminating. The former, a suspect pair of Spitfires (in fact, almost certainly Hurricanes), were claimed by two Feldwebeln of 9. *Staffel* – one of them Hans Stechmann – over Kent on 1 December 1940. The latter, identified as a Blenheim and credited to Hauptmann Hans von Hahn, the *Gruppenkommandeur* of I./JG 3, was brought down off the French coast on 10 January 1941 – proof, if proof were needed, that the tide of battle in the west had finally turned. The mass of the Luftwaffe could no longer operate over southern England by day, and now the Channel *Jagdgeschwader* found themselves being forced into a more defensive posture as the RAF started its 'lean into France'.

This 'lean' had begun with a series of raids, codenamed 'Circuses', each comprising a small number of Blenheim IV bombers heavily escorted by fighters. It was the first such 'Circus' – consisting of six Blenheim IVs protected by no fewer than 72 fighters flown on 10 January 1941 against an ammunition dump to the south of Calais – that had purportedly given Hauptmann von Hahn his 12th victory northeast of Nieuport on that date. British sources state that all six bombers got back safely, however, the only loss being a single Hurricane.

Less than a month later, however, 'Circus' No 3 did not fare so well. Although none of the 12 Blenheim IVs sent to bomb St Omer airfield on 5 February was lost, nine of their escorting fighters failed to return. St Omer happened to be the home of Hans von Hahn's I./JG 3, and it seems reasonable to assume that it was this unit which inflicted most of the losses suffered by the RAF. In all, I. and III. *Gruppen* were credited with a total of 14 British fighters destroyed – eight Spitfires and six Hurricanes – for just one of their own machines damaged.

In a series of vicious dogfights, which lasted a good 30 minutes and extended across the Pas-de-Calais and beyond, three pilots (all of them future Knight's Cross winners) managed to notch up their fifth victories. Two NCOs of 2. *Staffel*, Oberfeldwebel Robert Olejnik and Feldwebel Hans Ehlers, downed a Spitfire apiece northwest of St Omer, while 9. *Staffel's* Feldwebel Otto Wessling caught a Hurricane to the west of Calais. In addition to a number of first time claimants, two other pilots were able to boost their existing scores. Leutnant Helmut Meckel, the *Staffelkapitän* of 2./JG 3, took his into double figures with a pair of Spitfires (his tenth and eleventh victories) shot down in the St Omer area.

Meanwhile, some 30 kilometres to the west, close to III./JG 3's airfield at Desvres, Hauptmann Walter Oesau claimed his first kill since assuming command of the *Gruppe* nearly three months earlier. The Hurricane he brought down as the raiders retired towards the coast raised his personal total to 40, and resulted in the award of the Oak Leaves the following day.

Portrayed here wearing the Knight's Cross won in July 1944 when a hauptmann and *Gruppenkommandeur* of I./JG 1, Feldwebel Hans Ehlers scored the fifth of his 14 victories with JG 3 northwest of St Omer on 5 February 1941

Another future Knight's Cross winner in action against the RAF's 'Circus' No 3 of 5 February 1941 was the then Leutnant Helmut Meckel, the *Staffelkapitän* of 2./JG 3, who claimed a brace of Spitfires to take his score to 11. Neither Meckel nor Ehlers (opposite) was to survive the war

The successful action of 5 February 1941 was a fitting swansong to JG 3's first stint on the Channel coast. Less than a fortnight later the *Geschwader* began withdrawing to bases in the Reich, where it was to exchange its now decidedly war-weary *Emils* for brand new Bf 109Fs. The unit returned to its old stamping grounds around the St Omer region of northeastern France early in May 1941. JG 3 was not destined to remain here for long, however. During the course of the next four weeks of intermittent cross-Channel sparring the honours were just about even. Despite being mounted on their new, improved, *Friedrichs*, the *Geschwader's* pilots were only able to claim 14 enemy aircraft destroyed for the loss of 13 of their own number (killed, missing or captured). I./JG 3 fared the worst of all. Its two successes cost the unit six pilots and eight aircraft. Among those who failed to return during this period was six-victory ace Oberleutnant Gerd Sprenger, the *Kapitän* of 1. *Staffel*, who was declared missing after tangling with British fighters over the Channel on 16 May.

In some recompense for its single loss, II. *Gruppe's* sole claim – for a Spitfire downed off Dunkirk on 7 May – had been made by Oberleutnant Gordon Gollob, the *Staffelkapitän* of 4./JG 3. This was Gollob's first victory with the *Geschwader*, albeit his sixth overall. At the beginning of the war he had been a *Zerstörer* pilot with I./ZG 76 in Poland. After achieving 80 victories with JG 3, Gollob would subsequently be appointed *Kommodore* of JG 77. By August 1942 his score had climbed to 150, for which he received the Diamonds. Thereafter he served in a number of increasingly important staff positions, finally reaching the very top when he replaced the disgraced Adolf Galland as *General der Jagdflieger* in January 1945.

But to return to the Channel front in the late spring of 1941, Hauptmann Walter Oesau's III./JG 3 was the most successful of the three *Gruppen* at this time. The unit countered its six losses by claiming nine RAF fighters and two Blenheim IV bombers destroyed. Among the former were the Spitfire and Hurricane shot down over the Straits of Dover by the *Kommandeur*, which had taken 'Gulle' Oesau's personal tally to 42. These proved to be the last victories that JG 3 would claim over northwest Europe for more than two years. It would be the summer of 1943 before the *Geschwader* returned to the area to take its place as part of the Defence of the Reich organisation. In the interim it was to experience two very different operational environments – the snowy wastes of the USSR, including the frozen hell that was Stalingrad, and the desert sands of North Africa.

CHAPTER THREE

BARBAROSSA – AN ABUNDANCE OF ACES

When the men and machines of JG 3 departed the Pas-de-Calais for a second time in June 1941 and started to stage eastwards for German-occupied Poland, the *Geschwader* was embarking upon an entirely new chapter in its career – the invasion of the Soviet Union. Nor was the change purely geographical. The scale and tempo of the operations to come would be unlike anything its members, air- and groundcrew alike, had ever experienced before.

To date, after more than a year of near continual campaigning against the Western Allies, the pilots of JG 3's three *Gruppen* had slowly and laboriously amassed a combined total of almost 400 enemy aircraft destroyed. In the next four months alone, they would be credited with more than three times that number of Soviet machines shot down. Personal scores would begin to soar rapidly to heights that would have been unimaginable only weeks earlier. Between June and October 1941 more than 50 pilots would reach the five-victory mark. Multiple daily kills would become almost commonplace as many individuals climbed steadily into double figures. Two would exceed 80 and one – *Geschwaderkommodore* Major Günther Lützow – would top the century mark.

With such a multitude of claims made during engagements fought over often featureless and unfamiliar terrain, and against what was then still a largely amorphous and unknown enemy (many pilots initially had great difficulty in identifying the types of enemy aircraft they were shooting down), it is clearly impossible to itemise every victory and chart the emergence of each newly fledged five-victory ace. Yet even against this background of more than 1200 claims in just four months (sometimes as many as 20 or 30 in a single day), certain names began to stand out above the others – those referred to in Luftwaffe circles as the true *Experten*. It was

Reflecting the more relaxed atmosphere of an operational station 'in the field', Hauptmann Walter Oesau, the *Kommandeur* of III./JG 3, reports in shirt-sleeve order to his GOC, *General der Flieger* Robert Ritter von Greim, during the latter's visit to Moderovka on the second day of *Barbarossa*. Note Oesau's 'White Double Chevron' in the background

Oberleutnant Robert Olejnik, the *Staffelkapitän* of 1./JG 3, is widely recognised as having brought down the very first Soviet aircraft (an I-16) of the war in the east. It was his sixth victory to date, but this shot of him being congratulated by his chief mechanic, Feldwebel Mackert, was not taken on that occasion, as other photos in the same series show Olejnik's rudder bearing 21 kill bars. Another minor oddity is that on the original photograph a Knight's Cross is visible around Olejnik's neck. Records indicate, however, that he did not receive this decoration until victory No 32

to be the *Geschwader's* most successful period of the entire war, both in terms of the number of enemy aircraft destroyed and in the number of decorations conferred upon its pilots. Between 9 July and 4 November 1941 no fewer than 19 Knight's Crosses and higher would be awarded to JG 3.

By the third week of June 1941 JG 3's three *Gruppen* were deployed on fields some 100 kilometres to the southeast of Lublin, close to the demarcation line between German- and Soviet-occupied Poland. The *Geschwader* now comprised the fighter component of *General der Flieger* von Greim's V. *Fliegerkorps*, itself a part of *Luftflotte* 4 – the air fleet that was responsible for covering the southern sector of the invasion front. V. *Fliegerkorps'* specific role was to provide air support for *Panzergruppe* 1's advance on the Ukrainian capital Kiev.

The events of 22 June 1941, the opening day of Operation *Barbarossa*, are too well known to warrant detailed repetition here. Suffice it simply to say that by its end the Luftwaffe's pre-emptive strikes on the Red Air Force's frontier airfields had cost the Soviets a staggering 336 aircraft shot down and close on 1500 destroyed on the ground!

JG 3's part in the day's proceedings netted its pilots a total of 25 confirmed aerial victories. The Bf 109s of I. *Gruppe* were the first in action. They had taken off from Zamosc-Dub at around 0340 hrs to carry out a series of low-level attacks on six enemy fields in the Lemberg (Lvov) region, but they claimed their first victim well before reaching the target area. In fact, the single Soviet I-16 fighter that Oberleutnant Robert Olejnik, the *Kapitän* of 1. *Staffel*, brought down almost immediately after crossing the border was not just JG 3's first success of the day, it is now widely accepted that Olejnik's kill – his sixth to date – was the very first casualty of the air war in the east. Seven other pilots from I./JG 3 were also credited with kills as the day progressed.

III. *Gruppe*, however, was not so lucky. It too had started out by attacking Soviet airfields shortly after 0400 hrs, but had then been employed on bomber escort duties. The unit's sole success on this historic day had been credited to an NCO pilot of 7. *Staffel*, the I-15 biplane being the first victory for Unteroffizier Helmut Rüffler. By war's end Oberfeldwebel Rüffler would be wearing the Knight's Cross, having raised his final score to 98.

Rüffler's single success hardly compensated for the loss of 12-victory Oberleutnant Willy Stange, however, the *Staffelkapitän* of 8./JG 3 being forced to land behind enemy lines after his 'Black 10' was damaged by flak. Although other members of the *Staffel* saw him climb apparently uninjured out of his machine, Stange was quickly captured and killed by a group of Soviet soldiers.

The *Geschwaderstab* also claimed a single victory on 22 June. Not surprisingly, it fell to the guns of *Kommodore* Major Günther Lützow. Identified as an 'I-18' (in all probability a MiG-3), it was Lützow's 19th kill of the war. A brace of SB-2 twin-engined bombers 24 hours later took him to 21. After a single I-153 fighter the following day, Lützow added three more medium bombers on 26 June. This marked the start of a steady succession of multiple kills – on some days as many as four, and on 8 October five – that 'Franzl' Lützow would continue to amass throughout the *Geschwader's* first stint on the eastern front. During that time the *Stab* was credited with exactly 100 enemy aircraft destroyed, and the *Kommodore* was responsible for 83 of them, taking his overall total to 101 and earning him the Oak Leaves and the Swords in the process.

Major Günther Lützow was without question the *Geschwader's* most successful pilot during this stage of its operational history, but others were running him close. And none closer than II. *Gruppe's* Hauptmann Gordon Gollob.

II./JG 3 had been the highest scoring of the three *Gruppen* on the opening day of *Barbarossa*. Among its 15 victories were firsts for future Knight's Cross recipients Oberleutnant Walther Dahl of the *Gruppenstab* and Leutnant Hans Fuss of 4. *Staffel*. An I-153 took Oberleutnant Franz Beyer, also of the *Gruppenstab*, to five and an I-16 provided Gordon Gollob, the *Staffelkapitän* of 4./JG 3, with his seventh. But Hauptmann Lothar Keller outdid them all, the *Gruppenkommandeur's* four victories (a pair each of I-16s and I-153s) raising his total to 20.

A year earlier, during the *Blitzkrieg* against France, 20 victories would have meant an almost automatic Knight's Cross, but times, and the criteria for the awarding of decorations, were already changing. Lothar Keller did not get a Knight's Cross. Nor did he get any more victories. He was killed four days later. There is, however, some uncertainty regarding the exact circumstances that led to his death. All sources agree that he lost his life in a mid-air collision with another (unidentified) Luftwaffe aircraft. However, some references state that he was flying a *freie Jagd* sweep in his fighter at the time, whilst others maintain that he was piloting a Fieseler Storch on a local reconnaissance flight. The latter may well have been the case, for the *Gruppe* had been ordered to transfer forward to a new field on this date, and the *Kommandeur* was perhaps checking out the lie of the land in preparation for the move.

Whatever the true facts, Keller's loss appears to have led to a change of heart on the part of the authorities, for on 9 July he would become the first member of JG 3 to be honoured with a posthumous Knight's Cross.

23 June saw a repeat performance by II. and III. *Gruppen*, who again shot down exactly the same number of enemy aircraft as the day before – 15 and 1, respectively. In contrast, I./JG 3 more than doubled its opening day's score by claiming 19 Soviet bombers. Although this haul produced no new aces for the *Gruppe*, a quartet of Tupolev SB-2s did take Oberleutnant Robert Olejnik's tally up into double figures.

Geschwaderkommodore Major Günther Lützow pictured in the opening weeks of the war against the Soviet Union (prior to his being awarded the Oak Leaves on 20 July 1941). Note the distinctive 'White Triple Chevron' adorning his Bf 109F-2

The next two days resulted in a further 37 Soviet aircraft being added to the *Geschwader's* collective scoreboard and the emergence of six more aces, including future Oak Leaves winner Oberleutnant Viktor Bauer, currently the *Staffelkapitän* of 9./JG 3.

On 26 June the action flared up again with a vengeance. It was on this date that I./JG 3 enjoyed – if 'enjoyed' be the right word – its most successful day of the entire war by claiming a staggering 31 enemy machines shot down! The majority of the *Gruppe's* victims were hacked from the waves of medium bombers that the Soviets were sending over in their desperate attempts to halt the German advance. Somewhat surprisingly, this slaughter produced only one new ace – an Ilyushin DB-3 gave 1. *Staffel's* Feldwebel Detlev Lüth his fifth. Nevertheless, both Oberleutnant Robert Olejnik and Hauptmann Hans von Hahn were able to claim multiple victories, five DB-3s for Olejnik (thereby making him another 'ace-in-one-day') and a brace of DB-3s, plus a single SB-2, for *Gruppenkommandeur* von Hahn.

Robert Olejnik not only scored the first aerial victory of *Barbarossa*, he also became JG 3's first Russian Front 'five-in-one-day' ace on 26 June 1941 (beating Oberleutnant Viktor Bauer of 9./JG 3 by a matter of mere hours). He is seen here (right) – still on the Channel front – explaining his tactics to a Luftwaffe war correspondent while, in the background, fellow-*Staffelkapitän* Oberleutnant Helmut Meckel of 2./JG 3 (in flying overalls) looks on with some amusement

Although III./JG 3's total tally for the day was nine fewer than I. *Gruppe's* spectacular haul, it too achieved some impressive individual results. Hauptmann Walter Oesau's four (a trio of SB-2s and an I-15 fighter) raised his personal score to 48 – by far the highest in the *Geschwader* at that time – while Oberleutnant Viktor Bauer ran Robert Olejnik a close second by also claiming 'five-in-one-day'. Olejnik's five are believed all to have gone down before noon, whereas the last of Bauer's five bombers – a DB-3, which he chased and caught some 80 kilometres inside Soviet territory – was not logged until 1625 hrs.

In comparison to the performances of I. and III. *Gruppen*, the day's bag for II./JG 3 was positively sparse. And the dozen DB-3s with which its pilots *were* credited did little to make up for the loss of their *Gruppenkommandeur*, Hauptmann Lothar Keller, as previously described.

With the war in the east still only five days old, unit and individual scores were already beginning to escalate at a rate never before imagined, let alone experienced. Against such a background the accumulation of five victories – which in British and American eyes constituted the definition of an ace (and which will continue to be used here) – became almost meaningless. Before the *Geschwader's* first spell of duty in Russia came to an end early in November, over 40 more of its pilots would have claimed their fifth kills. Many of them then climbed rapidly into double figures, soon surpassing the once seemingly unattainable 20-victory mark. A select few went even further. On the last day of June, for example, Hauptmann Walter Oesau's 11th kill since being brought in to take command of III. *Gruppe* made him the first half-centurion to serve in the ranks of JG 3 (his first 39 having been gained with I./JG 20 and III./JG 51).

Luzk, 6 July 1941, and I./JG 3's *Gruppenkommandeur* Hauptmann Hans von Hahn (right) surveys his record of successes to date . . .

The *Geschwader* continued to support the ground forces' drive eastwards throughout July. During that month JG 3 was credited with just over 500 enemy aircraft destroyed, almost exactly half that total falling to 'Gulle' Oesau's III. *Gruppe* alone. The bulk of their successes were made up of twin-engined bombers, which the Soviets were still sacrificing in prodigious numbers. In addition to their defensive duties, JG 3's pilots also carried out numerous *freie Jagd* sweeps as well.

July 1941 brought the *Geschwader* its first clutch of eastern front awards. These included three Knight's Crosses, the first of which was conferred upon Hauptmann Hans von Hahn, the *Gruppenkommandeur* of I./JG 3, on 9 July for his 21 victories. Eighteen days later the next went to Oberleutnant Robert Olejnik, the *Kapitän* of von Hahn's 1. *Staffel*, for 32 victories. And on 30 July Oberleutnant Viktor Bauer, the *Staffelkapitän* of 9./JG 3, received his for 34 victories.

The month had also seen two other even more prestigious awards. Having claimed his 50th on 30 June, Hauptmann Walter Oesau reached his 60th on 8 July, his 70th three days later and his 80th just four days after that. This amazing run culminated in another 'first' on 15 July – the immediate award of the first Swords to be won by a member of the *Geschwader*. And on 20 July – the day that he claimed a pair of 'single-engined bombers' (possibly early model Il-2 *Shturmoviks*) to take his score to 42 – *Kommodore* Major Günther Lützow was awarded the Oak Leaves.

'Gulle' Oesau, incidentally, was to claim six more victories as *Kommandeur* of III./JG 3 before being posted away to become a *Geschwaderkommodore* himself – of the famous JG 2 'Richthofen' on the Channel front.

. . . which was also applied with equal care to the starboard side of his machine's rudder. The three balloon symbols are self-explanatory, as are the three half-length bars denoting aircraft destroyed on the ground (one western, two Russian). The upper row of ten aerial victories (commencing top right with a Hurricane brought down during the 'Phoney war') were all claimed while von Hahn was a member of JG 53. The remaining 14 (five RAF and nine Soviet) are his current 'bag' as *Kommandeur* of I./JG 3 – the last two a pair of DB-3s accounted for on 6 July 1941

Groundcrew of 9./JG 3 stop work on Leutnant Helmut Mertens' 'Yellow 6' to wave up at another F-2 as it circles Polonnoye prior to landing. Word must already have got around . . .

. . . that one of the three I-153s just shot down by Oberfeldwebel Hans Stechmann on this 15 July 1941 is the *Geschwader's* 1000th victory of the war! Little wonder that Stechmann's 'Yellow 4' is mobbed as it taxies to a halt

Inevitably, there were casualties too. Among the dozen pilots of JG 3 reported killed or missing during July 1941 were four more of the unit's newly fledged aces. II. *Gruppe* lost two such pilots within the space of 48 hours. 6. *Staffel's* Unteroffizier Horst Beyer, whose fifth victory had been a Petlyakov Pe-2 claimed on 28 June, was himself brought down and killed south of Kiev on 11 July. The fate of Oberleutnant Karl Faust, the *Staffelkapitän* of 4./JG 3 (whose fifth had also been a Pe-2, downed on 29 June), was even more tragic. Fired at in error by a Luftwaffe Ju 88, he was forced to land his damaged 'White 5' behind enemy lines on 12 July, only to be captured and shot by Soviet troops.

I./JG 3 also lost two of its new aces, both from 2. *Staffel* and both of whom had happened to claim their fifth kills (an I-16 apiece) on the same day (12 July) at exactly the same time (0740 hrs). Oberfeldwebel Hermann Kniewasser, having added a sixth to his total in the interim, was killed while attacking a group of enemy bombers on 17 July. And on the last day of the month Unteroffizier Günther Schulz, with his score still standing at five, was brought down by flak some 70 kilometres to the south of Kiev.

With the ground forces now closing in on the Ukrainian capital, August witnessed a marked reduction in the *Geschwader's* activities. They were credited with fewer than 250 enemy aircraft destroyed – less than half the previous month's total. A dozen more new aces had, however, emerged before August was out. All but two of them came from the ranks of II./JG 3, including future Oak Leaves recipients Unteroffizier Leopold 'Poldi' Münster and Oberleutnant Walther Dahl of later *Sturmgruppe* fame.

The month also saw four new Knight's Cross winners. All were *Staffelkapitäne*, three of whom were decorated on the same day. Oberleutnant Helmut Meckel, the *Kapitän* of 2. *Staffel*, had claimed his 25th, and last, victory north of Kiev back on 11 July. Shortly afterwards he had been taken off ops due to a severe illness. His place was taken by 27-victory Oberleutnant Max Bucholz. Both men received the Knight's Cross on 12 August.

The third *Staffelkapitän* to be presented with the award on that date, 7./JG 3's Oberleutnant Kurt Sochatzy, was already a prisoner of the Soviets. The right wing of Sochatzy's 'White 9' had been torn off when he was rammed by an I-16 during a dogfight over Kiev on 3 August. Sochatzy was credited with the I-16 (or one of its fellows) as his 38th, and last, victory. He himself was forced to take to his parachute and survived both the descent and his subsequent eight years of Russian captivity. He was the only JG 3 ace to be lost in August 1941. The month's fourth, and final, Knight's Cross went to Oberleutnant Franz Beyer, the *Kapitän* of 8. *Staffel*, although references differ as to whether his exact score at the time was standing at 31 or 32.

In September the *Geschwader's* successes were halved yet again, falling to a total of just 123. This may have been due in some measure to Hauptmann Hans von Hahn's I./JG 3 being withdrawn from the eastern front in the middle of the month and returned to Magdeburg, in Germany, to rest and refit. A small detachment did remain behind in Russia until the end of October, however. This allowed Oberfeldwebeln Detlev Lüth, Ernst Heesen and Hans Ehlers to take their final scores with the *Geschwader* to 26, 19 and 14, respectively. In mid-December I./JG 3 would be transferred from Magdeburg to the Dutch coast to help strengthen that region's air defences against attack by the RAF. But Hauptmann von Hahn's *Gruppe* would claim no victories in its new area of operations before being redesignated II./JG 1 on 15 January 1942.

Meanwhile, for the two *Gruppen* remaining in Russia, it was very much business as usual. On 4 September the first two of the month's four Knight's Crosses were awarded. Both went to oberfeldwebeln of 9. *Staffel*, Georg Schentke and Hans Stechmann, and both were for a total of

Oberleutnant Max Bucholz, who had replaced the ailing Helmut Meckel as *Staffelkapitän* of 2./JG 3 on 15 July, received the Knight's Cross less than a month later for a score then standing at 27 (the last five all claimed on 13 July)

Pictured in happier times together with the pilots of his 7./JG 3, *Staffelkapitän* Oberleutnant Kurt Sochatzy (third from right) was also awarded the Knight's Cross on 12 August 1941 – but *in absentia*, as he had already been a prisoner of the Soviets for nine days by then

Pictured at Byelaya-Zerkov in the latter half of August 1941, Leutnant Detlev Rohwer of the *Gruppenstab* I./JG 3 poses proudly alongside the rudder of his *Friedrich*, which shows a total of 27 kills (plus six machines destroyed on the ground). No 28 – identified as an R-10 light attack and reconnaissance aircraft – was to go down southeast of Kremenchug on 7 September, but it would be 5 October before Leutnant Rohwer received the coveted Knight's Cross

30 victories. Another oberfeldwebel, Heinrich Brenner of 4./JG 3, was less fortunate three days later when he became the only ace lost to the *Geschwader* in September. Brenner's fifth had been one of the three SB-3s he had brought down in the space of just eight minutes on 17 August. His total had risen to 12 by the time he lost his life in a dogfight with I-16s south of Kremenchug on 7 September.

Despite the loss of Heinrich Brenner, II./JG 3 was by far the more successful *Gruppe* in September with 80 confirmed victories (against III./JG 3's 15). Three of the *Gruppe's* NCO pilots, Oberfeldwebeln Erwin Kortlepel and Alfred Heckmann and Unteroffizier Werner Lucas – the latter pair future Knight's Cross winners – all reached the 20 mark during the course of the month. And on 12 September *Gruppenkommandeur* Hauptmann Gordon Gollob claimed his 40th. Gollob, who had taken over at the head of II./JG 3 after the loss of Lothar Keller just four days into *Barbarossa*, was awarded the Knight's Cross on 18 September (for a score then standing at 42).

The other Knight's Cross presented on that date went to an oberleutnant of III. *Gruppe* whose total was less than half that of Gollob's. It seems clear from these two instances that not only were the criteria for the conferral of decorations steadily being raised, but that inconsistencies were beginning to creep in too. For fighter pilots the number of victories gained was an important, perhaps the overriding factor in the winning of awards, but it was no longer the only one. Qualities of leadership, for example, were also being taken into account by this stage of the war. And just as some posthumous Knight's Crosses were awarded to honour those killed in action, others – or so at least one historian has suggested – may well have been handed out as a form of 'consolation prize' to pilots whose promising operational careers had been brought to a premature end.

Pictured sometime during the late summer of 1941, Hauptmann Hans von Hahn, the *Kommandeur* of I./JG 3, is still apparently using the unusual *Stab* insignia inherited from Günther Lützow some 12 months earlier. Note the completely different 'Cockerel's head' personal insignia now carried by his F-2, however

Oberleutnant Winfried Schmidt was perhaps a case in point. Upon the outbreak of war he had been a member of II./JG 77. His first victory had been one of the luckless RAF Wellingtons brought down on 18 December 1939 during the now famous 'Battle of the German Bight'. Since joining III./JG 3 his varying fortunes had seen him wounded at least twice, add a further 18 enemy aircraft to his score and rise to become the *Kapitän* of 8. *Staffel*. But his final victory, over a DB-3 on 11 July 1941, had resulted in his again being wounded – this time so seriously that he was no longer fit for flying duties. He would spend the remainder of the war in various staff appointments.

Another tail with a tale to tell. Despite the indifferent quality of the original print, this photograph of Hauptmann Gordon M Gollob's rudder scoreboard clearly shows the Polish marking (top left) indicating his first victory. This, and the four RAF roundels next to it, are for aircraft all downed while Gollob was a member of ZG 76. The fifth, and final, RAF roundel – for a Hurricane shot down into the Channel on 7 May 1941 – was his first victory with JG 3. It is followed by 27 Soviet stars, the last five of them for machines all claimed on 21 August

On 19 September, 24 hours after the announcement of Gollob's and Schmidt's Knight's Crosses, the German 6. *Armee* took Kiev. For the next seven days one of the largest and bloodiest 'cauldron' battles of the war raged to the east of the Ukrainian capital. By the time it was over some two-thirds of a million Red Army troops had been taken prisoner and the Soviet southwest front had been torn wide open. In the immediate aftermath of the cauldron battle of Kiev JG 3 was detached from V. *Fliegerkorps* in the Ukraine and transferred up to II. *Fliegerkorps* on the central sector of the front. Here it was to support Operation *Taifun* (Typhoon), Army Group Centre's offensive against Moscow, which was launched on 2 October 1941.

It was thus over unknown territory that the *Geschwader's* last three aces of 1941 were to claim their fifth victories. The territory may have been new to them, but their opponents were all too familiar. Number five for Unteroffizier Karl-Heinz Wallrath of 8./JG 3 was a DB-3 brought down on 3 October. Two days later Leutnant Emil Bitsch, also of 8. *Staffel*, claimed a SB-3. And 24 hours after that, 6./JG 3's Leutnant Gustav Frielinghaus – like Bitsch a future Knight's Cross recipient – was credited with a Pe-2.

As in the previous month, II./JG 3 was again by far the highest scoring *Gruppe* in October, claiming 84 victories compared to III. *Gruppe's* 33. There was a good reason for this. While III./JG 3 remained on the Moscow front in the face of increasing Soviet resistance and ever-worsening weather (the first snows had fallen within days of the launch of *Taifun*), Hauptmann Gollob's II. *Gruppe* had been withdrawn from the central sector on 16 October and sent to the far south for temporary attachment to JG 77 – the *Geschwader* that was supporting 11. *Armee's* drive down through the Perekop Isthmus on to the Crimea.

Whether at the gates of Moscow or over the more clement Crimea, the final weeks of JG 3's initial spell of operations in the east were dominated by just two names. On 7 October *Geschwaderkommodore* Major Günther Lützow had taken his score to 80 with a DB-3 downed west of the Soviet capital. Three days later a pair of Pe-2s were numbers 90 and 91. And on 24 October a MiG-3 gave 'Franzl' Lützow his century. He was only the second pilot in the history of aerial warfare (after the legendary Werner Mölders) to achieve 100 victories!

Hauptmann Gordon M Gollob, *Gruppenkommandeur* of II./JG 3, wearing the Oak Leaves awarded on 26 October 1941 for his then overall total of 85 enemy aircraft destroyed (80 of them while serving with JG 3)

To the south Hauptmann Gordon Gollob, *Kommandeur* of II. *Gruppe*, therefore had some ground to make up – but he was doing so, fast. His 50th had gone down over the central sector on 5 October. His 60th, the second of three MiG-3s claimed on 17 October, was scored during the *Gruppe's* first day in action over the Crimea. Incredibly, his 70th followed just 24 hours later – the last of nine(!) MiGs claimed in a single day. It then took all of four more days for him to get his 80th.

These achievements earned both men high awards. Major Günther Lützow received his Swords on 11 October (for his then 92 victories) and Hauptmann Gollob's Oak Leaves followed on 26 October (for 85 victories). It was a fitting finale to the *Geschwader's* time in Russia – although 'Franzl' Lützow had managed to sneak in his 101st (another MiG-3) on 24 October before being officially taken off operations upon specific 'orders from above'. Werner Mölders had been similarly banned from further combat flying after reaching his century. At this (relatively early) stage of the war, the risk of handing a propaganda coup to the enemy by having a 100-victory ace lost in action still outweighed any operational considerations. It was a policy that would not survive for much longer.

It may be unfair, but after such stellar performances the last two Knight's Crosses won in this chapter of the unit's history come as something of an anti-climax. Both were awarded on 4 November. They went to Oberleutnant Georg Michalek, the *Staffelkapitän* of 4./JG 3, for a score of 36 and to 5./JG 3's Feldwebel Walter Ohlrogge for his 39. Very nearly 33 years of age, Ohlrogge was one of the oldest fighter pilots in the Luftwaffe, and certainly the oldest in his *Staffel*, where he was affectionately referred to as the *'Altmeister'*, or 'Old Master'.

II./JG 3 flew its last operations over the Crimea on 31 October. One of the two enemy machines downed during these final missions provided victory number 20 for Oberleutnant Heinrich Sannemann, a long-serving *Staffelkapitän*. Then, early in November, the *Gruppe* was ordered to hand its remaining dozen or so serviceable Bf 109s over to III./JG 77 and prepare for transfer back to the Reich. On the central sector III./JG 3 at Orel was likewise instructed to pass its aircraft over to JG 51 and make ready to return to Germany.

The last members of JG 3 to bid farewell to the eastern front in 1941 were Oberstleutnant Günther Lützow's *Geschwaderstab* (the *Kommodore's* promotion from major had come through on 29 October). By 8 November the *Stab* was based on a field just 120 kilometres to the southeast of Moscow. It was on this date that it was credited with the last of the 106 victories it had claimed since the start of *Barbarossa*. The twin-engined DB-3 that Leutnant Eckhardt Hübner downed close to the Soviet capital was his 19th kill while serving with the *Stab* in Russia, and it took his overall total to 31 – his opening 12 had been scored with III. *Gruppe*.

This marked the end of the first round in JG 3's war against the Soviet Union. It would not be long before the *Jagdgeschwader* returned, but when it did the unit would find conditions very different.

CHAPTER FOUR
MEDITERRANEAN INTERLUDE

It was only a matter of days after JG 3 had returned to Germany (*Geschwaderstab* and II. *Gruppe* to Wiesbaden-Erbenheim and III. *Gruppe* to Mannheim-Sandhofen) that Generaloberst Ernst Udet, the Luftwaffe's Quartermaster-General, committed suicide in Berlin. The normally ebullient Udet – World War 1 fighter ace, interwar stunt pilot and *bon viveur* – had been driven to take his own life by charges levelled at him from certain quarters that it was his policies alone which had cost the Luftwaffe victory in the Battle of Britain, and were preventing the speedy conquest of the Soviet Union.

The Nazi hierarchy quickly sought to cover up the true circumstances of Udet's death. His shooting himself with his own service pistol became 'lost his life while testing a new weapon'. The authorities then went even further by staging a grandiose state funeral, one result of which was the loss of *General der Jagdflieger* Werner Mölders, who was killed in an aeroplane crash while returning from a tour of the eastern front to attend the ceremony.

Nor did it end there. In an Order of the Day issued on 1 December 1941 headed 'Comrades of the Luftwaffe!', *Reichsmarschall* Hermann Göring paid fulsome tribute to Udet's personal commitment and 'selfless devotion to duty'. This paean of praise closed with the words;

'His fame is undying. That is why I am today fulfilling the task entrusted to me by the *Führer* and Supreme Commander of the Wehrmacht by conferring upon the *Jagdgeschwader* 3, in his name, the honour title *Jagdgeschwader* "Udet". This will ensure that the memory of one of the greatest in the Luftwaffe will be enshrined for all time.'

The only outward signs of this signal honour would be the cuff band bearing the legend '*Jagdgeschwader* Udet', which was to be worn by unit members on the right sleeve of their uniform jackets, and the new winged 'U' for Udet badge that would adorn their aircraft. Of far greater practical interest to all personnel that November and December was the arrival of their new complement of Bf 109Fs. Each machine was fitted with a sand filter. This could mean only one thing – having experienced the first snows of a Russian winter, the *Geschwader's* two *Gruppen* were now destined for the sunnier climes of the Mediterranean!

In fact, after the German ground offensive had been brought to a halt in front of Moscow late in 1941, the whole of II. *Fliegerkorps* was withdrawn from the central sector of the eastern front and transferred down to Sicily in preparation for a renewed assault on the Mediterranean island of Malta. Sicily was JG 3's intended destination too. But only II. *Gruppe* would make it that far. In Russia, the Red Army had not merely succeeded in stopping the German advance on Moscow. It had also launched a major winter offensive of its own in the south that soon began to threaten several important towns only recently captured by the

After a Russian winter, the warmer climes of the Mediterranean came as a very welcome change. With one of their tropicalised F-4s basking in the sun behind them, these three pilots of the newly titled II./JG 3 'Udet' discuss tactics at San Pietro, Sicily, in the early spring of 1942. Note the kapok life-jackets – essential garb for ops against the island of Malta

Germans, including Kharkov, which had fallen to the 6. *Armee* on 24 October. This escalating danger in the east necessitated a hurried change of plans by the Luftwaffe. And among the units affected was JG 3.

By the second week of January 1942 both II. and III. *Gruppen* were in the process of dismantling their aircraft for transport by rail down to Bari, on the heel of Italy, where they would be re-assembled for the onward flight to Sicily. It was while still at Bari in late January that III./JG 3 unexpectedly received orders to hand its Bf 109F-4/trops over to II. *Gruppe* and return forthwith to Messerschmitt's Wiener Neustadt factory to collect a fresh complement of non-tropicalised F-4s, prior to returning to the eastern front. This meant that the only part of JG 3 actually to operate over Malta would be II. *Gruppe* (which had also taken charge of the four machines of the *Geschwaderstab* that had arrived in Bari).

It was while still at Wiesbaden back in November 1941 that Hauptmann Gordon Gollob had departed to take up duties with the Luftwaffe's main test centre at Rechlin. His replacement at the head of II./JG 3 – or II./JG 3 'Udet', as it should now rightly be called – was Hauptmann Karl-Heinz Krahl, previously the *Gruppenkommandeur* of I./JG 2 'Richthofen'.

It was thus under Karl-Heinz Krahl that the *Gruppe* set out on the final leg of its journey to Sicily towards the end of January 1942. Based for a brief time at Comiso in the southeast, it subsequently moved to Sciacca, in the western part of the island. It was while here that the unit lost its only ace in the Mediterranean (quite literally!) when, on 13 February, nine-victory Leutnant Karlheinz Ponec of the *Gruppenstab* was reported missing after being forced to ditch in the sea due to engine damage.

Two days later, 6. *Staffel's* Unteroffizier Wolfgang Vogel was credited with the *Gruppe's* first Mediterranean kill – one of a small formation of Beaufighters that had just taken off from Malta en route to Egypt. It was a first for Wolfgang Vogel too, and he would go on to claim a further 21 enemy aircraft before being lost over Russia six months hence.

II./JG 3 'Udet' included a number of very experienced NCO pilots among its ranks. This impressive scoreboard, kicking off with a solitary Spitfire (claimed on 16 August 1940) followed by 42 Soviet stars, adorns the tail of Feldwebel Walter Ohlrogge's F-4/trop. But success over Malta was to elude the 'Old Master'

But it was from San Pietro, back in the southeast of Sicily, that II./JG 3 would see the bulk of what little action it was to be involved in during its brief interlude in the Mediterranean. The *Gruppe's* next success came on 22 February – the day of its move down to San Pietro. It was while escorting a trio of Ju 88 bombers to Malta on this date that 4. *Staffel's* Feldwebel Leopold Münster was able to claim a Hurricane, thereby taking his personal tally to 13. More than two weeks were to pass before another Ju 88 raid on Luqa airfield on 10 March gave Hauptmann Karl-Heinz Krahl the opportunity to score his first (and last) victory with JG 3. Although claimed as a Spitfire, Krahl's victim was in all likelihood another Hurricane.

Aircraft recognition was clearly not a strong point with the next claimant either, for Allied sources would suggest that the 'Blenheim' that Unteroffizier Michael Beikiefer of 6./JG 3 shot into the sea on 18 March was, in reality, one of Malta's famous reconnaissance Marylands. The unfortunate Beikiefer did not survive his victim for long. Just 48 hours later he too disappeared into the sea during a practice flight off Gela.

The *Gruppe's* fifth, and final, confirmed Mediterranean victory was a Spitfire downed over Malta on 26 March by 4./JG 3's Leutnant Joachim Kirschner. It was only his second kill to date, but he, like 'Poldi' Münster, also of 4. *Staffel*, would later rise to become one of the *Geschwader's* select band of Oak Leaves wearers and, in fact, emerge as its highest scorer of all with a final total of 175!

Oberleutnant Walther Dahl, *Staffelkapitän* of 4./JG 3, is obviously describing a recent encounter with the RAF. However, even he failed to make his mark in the Mediterranean – his claim for a Spitfire downed during a Stuka escort mission to Malta on 1 April 1942 was not allowed

II./JG 3's five Mediterranean successes cost it six pilots killed, missing or captured, plus another six wounded or injured. One of the three who became PoWs was Unteroffizier Josef Fritz, shot down in a dogfight with Kittyhawks south of Tobruk on 13 April during 6. *Staffel's* three-week deployment to Martuba, in Libya – 6./JG 3 was the only part of the *Gruppe* to actually see service in North Africa. The final loss of II./JG 3's sojourn in the sun was *Kommandeur* Hauptmann Karl-Heinz Krahl, who was brought down by light flak during a low-level strafing run over Malta on 14 April. Lacking the height to bail out, Hauptmann Krahl was killed instantly when his machine crashed inverted into a stone wall.

His role as *Gruppenkommandeur* was filled within 24 hours by the appointment of Hauptmann Kurt Brändle, hitherto the *Staffelkapitän* of 5./JG 3. With 35 kills already under his belt, Brändle proved to be the ideal man for the job. He would lead II./JG 3 back from the Mediterranean at the end of April, throughout the subsequent 15 months of increasingly bitter fighting on the eastern front and still be at its head – the longest serving *Kommandeur* in the *Gruppe's* entire history – when finally reported missing over the North Sea in late 1943.

6. *Staffel* was the only element of II. JG 3 to see service in North Africa. Among its pilots was the current eight-victory (and future Knight's Cross winner) Unteroffizier Franz Schwaiger. He is pictured here (on the left in tropical kit) in front of his desert-camouflaged 'Yellow 3', which he has named after his girlfriend Gisela

CHAPTER FIVE

GROWING SOVIET RESISTANCE

After its abortive foray down into the Mediterranean, JG 3 soon found itself back in action again over Russia. Now, however, the Red Air Force of early 1942 was no longer the disorganised, badly mauled and badly led opponent that it had been at the start of *Barbarossa*. The enemy was beginning to show signs of 'operational understanding and cohesion', often by copying the tactics employed by the Luftwaffe. The portly Polikarpovs of 1941 were rapidly disappearing from the front as new Soviet fighter regiments were formed and equipped with more modern aircraft. The Red Air Force still had a long way to go, but the writing was already clearly on the wall.

Despite this, the coming months on the eastern front were to mark not just the halfway point in the *Geschwader's* operational history, but, in terms of numbers of enemy aircraft destroyed, the very pinnacle of its whole combat career. Between mid-February 1942 and the end of July 1943 the pilots of the *Jagdgeschwader* 'Udet' would be credited with very nearly 4000 victories! During that time more than 100 new five-victory aces would be created, 30 members of JG 3 would become so-called 'semi-centurions' by reaching a total of 50 or more and eight of the unit's topmost *Experten* would take their individual scores into triple figures.

The first *Gruppe* to return to the Russian front was III./JG 3, whose progress southwards had been so abruptly terminated at Bari, on Italy's Adriatic coast. After a brief stopover at Jesau, in East Prussia, where personnel were issued with winter clothing and equipment, it was despatched post-haste to the northern sector of the front. Here, another Soviet offensive was threatening to split open the boundary between Army Groups Centre and North. Arriving at Soltsy, a field close to Lake Ilmen, in the second week of February 1942, the *Gruppe's* immediate task in the days ahead was to escort and protect the Luftwaffe transport aircraft airlifting supplies into the Demyansk pocket, where almost 100,000 German troops had been surrounded by the Red Army.

It was to prove quite a costly undertaking. By the end of March III./JG 3 had lost six of its pilots, half of them aces. The first to go down was five-victory Unteroffizier

A Yak-4 shot down in the Demyansk area on 12 March 1942 made a semi-centurion out of Oberleutnant Franz Beyer, the *Staffelkapitän* of 8./JG 3 . . .

Karlheinz Wallrath of 8. *Staffel*. On 13 February, only the third day of operations over Demyansk, he had fallen victim to return fire from a group of Pe-2 medium bombers he was attacking to the east of the pocket. The other two, both of 7. *Staffel*, failed to return from a *freie Jagd* sweep to the south of Lake Ilmen, midway between Soltsy and Demyansk, on 28 March. One was Feldwebel Rudolf Berg, a promising NCO with 17 kills already to his credit. The other was Leutnant Eckhardt Hübner, who had rejoined III. *Gruppe* after claiming 19 victories while serving with the *Geschwaderstab* under 'Franzl' Lützow during the latter half of 1941, and had added another 28 since (the last two on the morning of the day he and Berg had subsequently set off on their ill-fated *freie Jagd* mission).

Nevertheless, III./JG 3's successes in the battle for Demyansk – nearly 175 kills in total – far outweighed these painful losses. During the course of the battle a handful of relative newcomers to the *Gruppe* had claimed their all-important fifth victories, four veterans (including the luckless Hübner) had taken their personal scores beyond 40 and two of the *Gruppe's Staffelkapitäne* had become semi-centurions. The 50th for 8./JG 3's Oberleutnant Franz Beyer was reportedly a Yak-4 high-speed bomber, something of a *rara avis*, which he claimed in the Demyansk area on 12 March. And it was just over three weeks later, on 4 April, that an unwary LaGG-3 fighter provided 9. *Staffel's* Oberleutnant Viktor Bauer with his half-century.

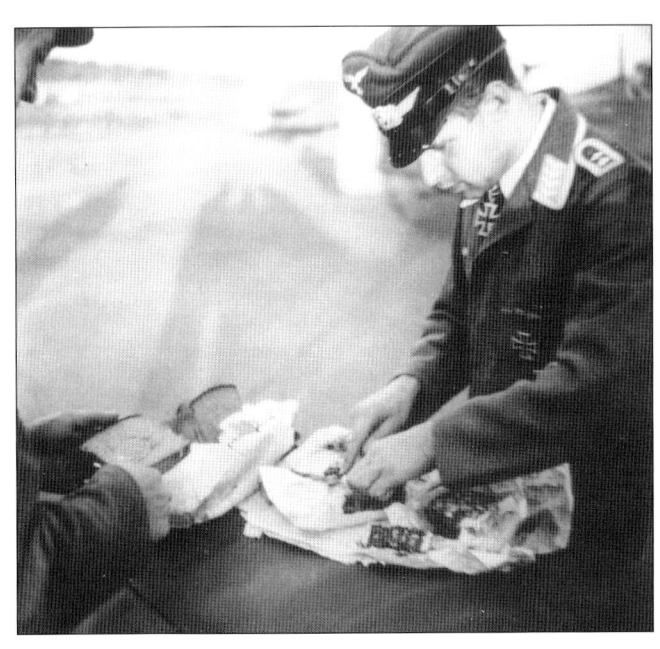

The battle of Demyansk came to an end on 21 April 1942 when a relief force finally managed to fight its way through to the men of the trapped II. *Armeekorps*. But by that time III./JG 3 had already left the scene, the *Gruppe* having departed Soltsy several days earlier for Wiesbaden-Erbenheim, where it was to spend the next month resting and re-equipping. It was while at Wiesbaden that the *Gruppe* was awarded its next trio of Knight's Crosses. One went posthumously to Leutnant Eckhardt Hübner on 3 May. On the same date 9. *Staffel's* Oberfeldwebel Eberhard von Boremski was decorated for his 43 victories, and just six days later another of the *Gruppe's* veteran NCOs, Oberfeldwebel Hans Schleef of 7./JG 3, received his for a score currently standing at 41.

. . . while fellow-*Staffelkapitän* Oberleutnant Viktor Bauer of 9./JG 3 (facing camera) attained his half-century by despatching a LaGG-3 south of Staraya Russa on 4 April

Franz Beyer and Viktor Bauer had both won their Knight's Crosses during the opening round of JG 3's war against the Soviet Union. The first member of the *Jagdgeschwader* 'Udet' to be decorated after the unit's return to the eastern front early in 1942 was 9. *Staffel's* Oberfeldwebel Eberhard von Boremski, who is pictured here using the tailplane of his machine as a handy work surface to prepare a round of tasty *Blutwurst* sandwiches!

The next *Gruppe* of JG 3 to arrive in Russia touched down at Kharkov on 26 April, only a week or so after III./JG 3 had returned to the Reich. Unlike Soltsy, Kharkov was on the southern sector – the *Geschwader's* old stamping grounds of the 1941 campaign. As such it should have been much more familiar territory, but this was not the case, for the *Gruppe* in question was the new I./JG 3, only recently activated to replace Hauptmann von Hahn's original I. *Gruppe*, which was now operating in the west as II./JG 1. It had been formed primarily from a number of training units, and only those few members who had been transferred across from either II. or III./JG 3 to provide the new unit with a small core of combat-experienced pilots had seen any previous service on the eastern front. Two such men were the *Gruppenkommandeur*, Hauptmann Georg Michalek, hitherto the *Staffelkapitän* of 4./JG 3, who already had 37 enemy machines to his credit, and 28-victory Oberfeldwebel Otto Wessling, previously of 9. *Staffel*.

It was not long before I. *Gruppe* was joined in the Ukraine by the rest of JG 3 'Udet'. The *Geschwaderstab*, under Oberstleutnant Lützow, arrived on 19 May. Major Kurt Brändle's II./JG 3, fresh from three weeks rest and recuperation at Pilsen, flew in on the same day. And just 24 hours later a rejuvenated III. *Gruppe* returned from Wiesbaden led by its new *Gruppenkommandeur*, Major Karl-Heinz Greisert (previously the *Kommandeur* of II./JG 2 'Richthofen').

With the *Stab* and all three *Gruppen* deployed on neighbouring fields around Kharkov, the stage was now set for JG 3's final 14 months of operations on the Russian front. In that time its pilots would witness the German defeat at Stalingrad and the titanic tank battle of Kursk – turning points not just of the campaign in the east, but of the entire war. The *Geschwader* was to find itself heavily engaged in both events, losing some 50 aces – both newly fledged and veteran – during this final period in Russia.

Despite their swingeing losses, and irrespective of how disastrously the war on the ground was going, the pilots of JG 3 continued to take a steady, and at times almost prohibitive, toll of the Red Air Force. Given the sheer weight of numbers involved – the nearly 4000 enemy aircraft destroyed, the emergence of 100+ new aces and more than a few personal scores climbing into three figures – it is again impossible to itemise all the victories achieved and losses suffered throughout this period. Yet

The rudder of Eberhard von Boremski's 'Yellow 4' displays the 43 victory markings that earned him the Knight's Cross on 3 May. The machine wears the 'amended' desert finish typical of the *Friedrichs* taken on charge by both I. and III. *Gruppen* during their refurbishment early in 1942. The identity of the rather uncomfortable-looking groundcrewman on the far left is not recorded, but the four 9. *Staffel* pilots pictured here are, from the left, Leutnant Rolf Diergardt (perched on cockpit sill), Oberfeldwebeln Georg Schentke and Eberhard von Boremski and *Staffelkapitän* Viktor Bauer (sitting on rear fuselage)

Despite the poor quality of this Soviet photograph, 9. *Staffel's* 'Yellow 9', which forced-landed behind enemy lines on 29 May, is also clearly wearing the three-tone ex-desert camouflage finish. One minor mystery, though – the rudder plainly shows four victory bars, yet pilot Gefreiter Adalbert Kuhn's score was standing at *seven* at the time of his capture

Oberstleutnant Günther Lützow (left) hands over command of the *Jagdgeschwader* 3 'Udet' to Hauptmann Wolf-Dietrich Wilcke . . .

...before giving one final salute as he prepares to leave the eastern front to take up an appointment on the staff of the *General der Jagdflieger* in Berlin. Note the *Geschwader's* new 'winged U' badge on the cowling of the unit's Junkers W 34 hack

even against this backdrop, every *Gruppe* managed to produce certain individuals whose achievements placed them head and shoulders above their fellows.

Not surprisingly perhaps, the recently activated and mostly unblooded I./JG 3 gained far fewer kills than either II. or III. *Gruppe*. Nonetheless, it too was to produce its fair share of *Experten* as the unit played its part in supporting the ground forces' advance on Stalingrad.

The new *Gruppe's* very first victory had been the MiG-3 credited to *Kommandeur* Hauptmann Georg Michalek on 8 May. Over the coming weeks the names of Michalek and Oberfeldwebel Otto Wessling were to dominate I./JG 3's scoreboard as their successes mounted. On 22 June 1942, the first anniversary of *Barbarossa*, Wessling claimed four of the day's dozen victories compared to the *Kommandeur's* two. But Michalek retained the overall lead, and it was he who first got to 50 with the second of the trio of LaGG-3s he downed in the space of five minutes early on the morning of 5 July. Wessling reached his half-century just over a fortnight later, on 21 July, by despatching an Il-2 *Shturmovik*. And so the friendly rivalry between CO and NCO might have continued, had not Hauptmann Michalek been posted away to take up a training appointment the following month.

August also witnessed command changes at the head of the *Geschwader*. Although officially banned from combat flying, *Kommodore* Oberstleutnant Günther Lützow had somehow managed to claim two more Soviet fighters (taking his total to 103) before being elevated to the staff of the *General der Jagdflieger* on 11 August. His replacement was Hauptmann Wolf-Dietrich Wilcke, who had gained 38 victories and won the Knight's Cross serving with JG 53 prior to his being transferred to JG 3. Known throughout the Jagdwaffe as 'Fürst' ('Prince') – a reference not only to his patrician bearing, but also to his innate and almost paternal sense of responsibility towards those serving under him – Wolf-Dietrich Wilcke had already amassed another 48 kills flying as a member of the *Stab* JG 3 before being officially appointed *Geschwaderkommodore* on 12 August 1942.

Wilcke was to carry on very much as 'Franzl' Lützow had left off, piling up the kills with multiple daily victories. He reached his century on 6 September (which won him the Oak Leaves three days later). Nor did he stop there. Apparently the 100-victory ban that had seen both Mölders and Lützow taken off operations was no longer being enforced. By the time the *Geschwaderstab* retired from Russia in April 1943 'Fürst' Wilcke's score would be standing at 156.

Although a long way behind the *Kommodore*, the second most successful member of the *Geschwaderstab* during this time on the eastern front was Hauptmann Walther Dahl. He had taken over as *Geschwader*-Adjutant on 2 August – the day after the previous holder of that office, Hauptmann Friedrich-Franz von Cramon, had been brought down by flak over the River Don. With 17 victories already gained during his earlier service with II./JG 3, Dahl would add a further 34 while flying as adjutant to Hauptmann (later Major) Wilcke.

Hauptmann Kurt Brändle's II./JG 3, which had been the only *Gruppe* to see action in the Mediterranean, would now follow this up by becoming the most successful of JG 3's three *Gruppen* during their second stint on the Russian front. By its close II./JG 3 had been credited with more than 1500 Soviet aircraft destroyed.

In addition to the *Gruppenkommandeur*, II./JG 3 included within its ranks several other pilots whose scores were rapidly climbing towards the 50 mark. Hauptmann Brändle himself

Although he had been denied a victory in the Mediterranean, Hauptmann Walther Dahl would end his subsequent year's stint as *Geschwader*-Adjutant in Russia by becoming a semi-centurion, the pair of LaGG-3s he was to claim on 17 April 1943 taking his overall total to 51

Hauptmann Kurt Brändle, appointed *Gruppenkommandeur* of II./JG 3 after the loss of Karl-Heinz Krahl over Malta, had reached his 50th on 29 June 1942. When this photograph was taken only six weeks later he was just five short of his century, and 16 days away from the Oak Leaves

Oberleutnant Helmut 'Pitt' Mertens, the *Staffelkapitän* of 1./JG 3, joined the ranks of the semi-centurions on 1 August 1942 by bringing down a Yak-1 to the west of Stalingrad. A glass of champagne and a victor's garland were awaiting him when he landed back at Frolov

4./JG 3's Feldwebel Werner Lucas achieved a spectacular double on 20 August 1942 by claiming 'five-in-one-day' and becoming a semi-centurion at one and the same time! It was the start of a dramatic rise for the veteran NCO, who is pictured here as an oberleutnant and the *Kapitän* of 4. Staffel at Kharkov-Rogan in the summer of 1943, shortly before II./JG 3's return to the Reich

became the first semi-centurion by downing a Pe-2 on 29 June (he would be awarded the Knight's Cross two days later for a quoted 49 victories). Hot on Brändle's heels was Leutnant Hans Fuss, also of the *Gruppenstab*. Another obliging Pe-2 gave Fuss his 50th on 6 July.

For a while the pair remained neck and neck at the top of the *Gruppe's* scoreboard. They both claimed their 60th within a week of each other in mid-July, but then Brändle began to edge ahead. A Yak-1 took him to 80 on 3 August, and the first of a trio of Sukhoi Su-2 single-engined bombers brought down just five days later was number 90. Leutnant Fuss, now the *Kapitän* of 6. *Staffel*, got his 70th on 9 August. This earned him the Knight's Cross – announced on 23 August for a reported 60 victories, a total he had in fact reached back on 17 July! But on the very day of Fuss' award, Hauptmann Brändle attained his century, for which he would receive the Oak Leaves on 27 August.

August had also seen the emergence from the pack of three NCO pilots. Feldwebel Leopold 'Poldi' Münster of 4. *Staffel* had got his 40th, a LaGG-3, on 6 August. The second of a brace of I-16s downed on 18 August took Oberfeldwebel Alfred Heckmann of 5./JG 3 to 50. And 48 hours after that a single Il-2 *Shturmovik*, plus a quartet of Pe-2s (victories Nos 48 to 52), made both an 'ace-in-a-day' and a semi-centurion out of Werner Lucas, another Feldwebel of 4. *Staffel*, at one and the same time!

At the other end of the scoring scale a dozen or more members of II. *Gruppe* were just getting into their stride by claiming their fifth kills. Among them were two leutnants. Number five for 5./JG 3's Joachim Kirschner had been a MiG-3 shot down back on 29 May. And it was another fighter, a Yak-1, that had provided the fifth for Wolf Ettel of 4./JG 3 on 9 July. Like Kirschner, Leutnant Ettel would also later wear Oak Leaves. But whether tyro or *Experte*, all of Brändle's pilots were glad of the respite when, towards the end of August 1942, II./JG 3 was ordered back to Germany for another brief period of rest and recuperation.

GROWING SOVIET RESISTANCE

Major Karl-Heinz Greisert – seen here (left) talking to Oberfeldwebel Georg Schentke – had enjoyed a successful career with JG 2 'Richthofen' in the west prior to his appointment as *Gruppenkommandeur* of III./JG 3 'Udet' on 18 May 1942. He would claim ten victories during his two months' tenure of command, taking his final total to 33, before being killed in action on 22 July

This impressive display – 91 aerial victories, plus nine enemy aircraft destroyed on the ground (top row) – almost fills the rudder of the machine flown by Oberleutnant Viktor Bauer, the *Kapitän* of 9. *Staffel*. He would reach his century with the second of two Red Air Force Hurricanes downed on 25 July 1942. After being awarded the Oak Leaves and taking his total to 106, Viktor Bauer was taken off ops. He was the highest-scoring ace of JG 3 'Udet' to survive the war

In the meantime, III./JG 3 had been suffering rather more mixed fortunes. After its operations over the Demyansk pocket earlier in the year, it too was now back on the southern sector. With the cauldron battle to the southwest of Kharkov nearing its end, the *Gruppe* was first to spend several weeks in the Crimea before redeploying to the Donetz front to add its support to the ground advance on Stalingrad. It was here, on 22 July, that the unit lost its *Kommandeur* when Major Karl-Heinz Greisert – who had achieved ten victories since assuming command – was shot down during a low-level dogfight. He attempted to bail out, but was killed when his parachute failed to open in time.

Nor was Greisert the unit's only casualty. In fact, of the 16 aces lost to JG 3 over the Ukraine between May and August 1942, seven came from the ranks of III. *Gruppe* alone. Included among them were two of their current highest scorers. The first to fall was 39-victory ace Oberfeldwebel Rudolf Saborowski of 8./JG 3, who had been brought down while attacking a formation of fighter-escorted Pe-2s over the River Don on 8 July. Leutnant Heinrich *Graf* von Einsiedel, who had 35 enemy machines to his credit, was captured after forced-landing behind Soviet lines in the Stalingrad region on 30 August.

And things were about to get a whole lot worse. The location of von Einsiedel's forced-landing provides the clue. Exactly a week prior to his loss, spearheads of 16. *Panzerdivision* had reached the banks of the River Volga. On the last day of August 4. *Panzerarmee* launched its attack on Stalingrad from the southwest. By the first week of September the leading elements of 51. *Armeekorps* were threatening the airfield at Gumrak, less than 15 kilometres from the outskirts of the city. Fearing encirclement, Soviet Lt-Gen A I Lopatin had wanted to withdraw his troops back across the Volga and leave Stalingrad to its fate. He was immediately replaced by Lt-Gen V I Chuikov, who vowed to 'defend the city or die in the attempt'. Almost 15 months of near constant retreat by the Red Army had finally come to an end. On the southern sector German forces, both on the ground and in the air, were soon to notice the difference.

JG 3's leading scorers continued to go from strength to strength nonetheless. In September five of the *Geschwader's* pilots received Knight's Crosses for reaching their half-centuries (see Appendix 1 for details). Two of the five were members of III./JG 3, which despite its losses had produced a clutch of true *Experten*. Foremost amongst these had been Oberleutnant Viktor Bauer, the long-serving *Kapitän* of 9. *Staffel*, who had attained his century with the second of the four enemy machines (two of them identified as British-built Hurricanes) that he had shot down within the space of five minutes back on 25 July. This feat had resulted in his being awarded the Oak Leaves the following day. On 9 August Viktor Bauer had claimed another four victories – this time in just four minutes – but with far different results. He was promptly taken off ops to spend the rest of the war in command of a succession of training units.

It would appear that Bauer's designated successor at the head of 9./JG 3 lasted only a matter of hours in the post, for 29-victory Leutnant Rolf Diergardt was reported missing in action in the Stalingrad region on 11 August. He had, in turn, been replaced by Oberleutnant Wilhelm Lemke. At the time of his appointment Lemke was rapidly approaching the 50 mark. But there were others in III. *Gruppe* with scores even higher than this. After the departure of Viktor Bauer, the leading trio were all NCOs – Oberfeldwebeln Eberhard von Boremski, Walter Ohlrogge and Georg Schentke, each of whom had 70+ kills to his credit. And not far behind was Oberleutnant Franz Beyer, the *Staffelkapitän* of 8./JG 3, with a score of 66.

In September III./JG 3 was to produce two more semi-centurions, and again they were both veteran NCOs of the kind that made up the backbone of every successful Luftwaffe fighter unit.

By the middle of that month III. *Gruppe* was operating out of Pitomnik airfield, less than 20 kilometres from the centre of Stalingrad. 18 September was a particularly busy day for the unit. Even though the field itself was under sporadic artillery fire from the Red Army, III./JG 3 became heavily involved in actions to the north of the city, where its pilots claimed 27 Soviet aircraft shot down. All but ten of this impressive bag was made up of Il-2 *Shturmoviks*. And it was two of these heavily armoured machines that provided the 50th apiece for Feldwebeln Siegfried Engfer and Heinz Kemethmüller. Having achieved their half-centuries on the same day, the pair would also be awarded their Knight's Crosses on the same day – 2 October.

The successes were overshadowed, however, by two painful losses for the *Geschwader*. On 5 September, after claiming victory number 75 during a dogfight close to the Don, Oberfeldwebel Ohlrogge was hit by

The two inseparables – Feldwebeln Siegfried Engfer and Heinz Kemethmüller both got their 50th on the same day (18 September 1942) and received their Knight's Crosses on the same day (2 October 1942). They were then granted a short spell of leave, and are pictured here still together at the fighter pilots' rest centre at Bad Wiessee, south of Munich

a burst of fire in the cockpit. Although grievously wounded, the 'Old Master' managed to put his Bf 109 down in friendly territory. He would spend many months in hospital and not return to frontline duty until the spring of 1944.

Fate was even harder on 71-victory Leutnant Hans Fuss, the *Staffelkapitän* of 6./JG 3. II. *Gruppe* had only just returned from two weeks of rest and recuperation in the Reich, and was currently on brief deployment to the central sector when, on 14 September, Fuss' machine was also damaged in combat. With fuel draining from a ruptured tank, Leutnant Fuss nursed his crippled fighter back to base northwest of Vyazma. Just as he was approaching to land the engine cut, the Bf 109 instantly dropping a wing and hitting the ground. It then somersaulted several times, inflicting serious injuries on Hans Fuss. Despite immediate medical attention and the subsequent amputation of one leg, he died in hospital in Berlin on 10 November.

At Stalingrad meanwhile, the rapidly worsening weather and growing Soviet resistance were having their effect on the once-mighty German war machine. In JG 3's case this was evidenced by October's claims and casualty lists. For although these showed the emergence of three new semi-centurions (Unteroffizier Franz Schwaiger of I. *Gruppe* and Leutnant Joachim Kirschner and Feldwebel Leopold Münster of II. *Gruppe*), they also recorded the loss of another six of the *Geschwader's* aces.

November's figures would prove to be exactly the same. One of that month's trio of semi-centurions was Major Wolfgang Ewald, who had assumed command of III./JG 3 after the loss Major Karl-Heinz Greisert back in July. The other two were Leutnant Ludwig Häfner and Feldwebel Helmut Rüffler, both of I. *Gruppe*. But Ludwig Häfner, the *Kapitän* of 3. *Staffel*, was also to be among the six aces lost in November. He was reported missing in action after clashing with a large group of Soviet Yaks on 10 November, just ten days after being credited with his 50th. Leutnant Häfner would be honoured with a posthumous Knight's Cross on 21 December.

On the broader scene, however, the events of November 1942 were no mere re-run of the month that had gone before. In fact, they marked nothing less than the turning of the tide of the whole war on the eastern front. On 19 November the Red Army launched a massive counter-offensive to the north of Stalingrad that quickly tore a wide gap in the lines of the Rumanian 3rd Army. The following day a similar assault breached the sector to the south of the city being held by Rumania's 4th Army. By 23 November the Soviets had captured the vital supply bridge over the River Don at Kalach, some 70 kilometres to the west of Stalingrad. The twin armoured pincers encircling the city then snapped shut and nearly a third of a million German and Axis troops were surrounded and cut off.

9. *Staffel's* Oberfeldwebel Walter Ohlrogge – the 'Old Master' – was severely wounded on 5 September 1942. Portrayed here after being commissioned as a leutnant, he returned to flying duties after a lengthy convalescence but, as far as is known, achieved no further victories

The situation on the ground heralded immediate changes for JG 3 too. The *Geschwader* had spent the best part of the last five months providing support for the men of the 6. *Armee* as they fought their way towards, and into, Stalingrad. Now its task would be to prevent those same men from being starved into submission. With Hitler's refusal to countenance any suggestion of a withdrawal, the fate of the troops trapped within the shrinking Stalingrad perimeter rested entirely on supply by air. The bombastic Göring had confidently assured his *Führer* that the Luftwaffe's fleet of Ju 52/3m transport aircraft would be more than adequate to meet 6. *Armee's* daily needs – he was totally and criminally wrong, of course. But the failure of the Stalingrad airlift was through no lack of trying on the part of the Junkers (and Heinkel) transport *Gruppen* that actually had to fly the missions.

JG 3 could do little against the two major enemies faced by the crews of the transports – the atrocious weather conditions and the Soviet anti-aircraft batteries concentrated along the air corridors leading into Stalingrad. The *Geschwader* was, however, able to help combat the Red Air Force's attacks on the heavily laden transport machines ferrying supplies into and wounded out of the pocket.

Based since September at Pitomnik – now within the Stalingrad perimeter, and fast becoming 6. *Armee's* main supply base – *Stab*, I. and III. *Gruppen* were ideally located for such operations (II./JG 3 was currently on temporary deployment to Smolensk, on the central sector). But the isolated nature of their position was now making it increasingly precarious. Indeed, so precarious that JG 3's fighters soon had to be withdrawn and transferred to Morosovskaya, one of the two principal supply depot airfields some 180 kilometres to the southwest of Stalingrad. This was too far away to enable them to provide proper protection at Pitomnik, however, where the transports were at their most vulnerable to attack during their turnaround time on the ground.

The *Geschwader* was therefore tasked with setting up the so-called *Platzschutzstaffel* 'Pitomnik', or Pitomnik Airfield Defence Squadron. Commencing operations on 19 November, this *Staffel* was formed around a cadre of volunteer pilots from I. *Gruppe*, some half-dozen of whom would spend several days at a time at Pitomnik on a rotational basis. On 12 December their numbers were reinforced by a similar group of volunteers from II./JG 3, which had flown down from Smolensk, on the central sector, to join the rest of the *Geschwader* at the Morosovskaya complex.

At Pitomnik, the *Staffel's* dispersal point was on the far side of the snow-covered field from the transports' loading and unloading areas. Weather conditions permitting, it tried to keep at least one *Rotte* (section of two fighters) at constant readiness to counter sneak bombing and strafing raids by the enemy. This precaution, coupled with standing patrols in the immediate vicinity of the field, paid handsome dividends. Over the coming weeks I. and II./JG 3 would be credited with the destruction of close on 225 enemy machines, many of them Il-2 *Shturmovik* ground-attack aircraft brought down by the volunteer pilots of the *Platzschutzstaffel* over and around Pitomnik.

During the two months of the *Staffel's* existence, a number of its members added considerably to their existing scores. Feldwebel Gustav Dilling of 2./JG 3 took his personal tally from 21 to 38 during this period.

The same unit's Leutnant Georg Schentke, recently transferred across from III. *Gruppe* and with 71 victories already under his belt, went two better than Dilling by claiming a further 19. And Leutnant Franz Daspelgruber, the *Staffelkapitän* of 1./JG 3, was credited with 22 – the last (his 45th overall) being a LaGG-3 shot down just two days before the *Platzschutzstaffel* was forced to abandon Pitomnik.

It was II. *Gruppe* – whose volunteers served with the Pitomnik *Staffel* for little more than a month – that produced possibly the most successful pilot of all. Feldwebel Kurt Ebener of 4./JG 3 got his first with the *Staffel* (his 20th overall – another of the ubiquitous *Shturmoviks*) on 17 December. This was but the start of a rapid succession of victories, including a number of multiple daily kills – five on 19 December, four each on 30 December and 10 January 1943 and three on 12 January. He closed with a final four on 15 January, taking his Pitomnik total to 33!

Despite the Soviets' overwhelming air superiority and the terrible weather conditions, the volunteers suffered remarkably light casualties. An NCO of II. *Gruppe* was slightly wounded when enemy flak forced him to make an emergency landing north of Pitomnik on 17 December. On the same day Oberleutnant Karl-Heinz Langer, the *Gruppen*-Adjutant of III./JG 3 and one of the few III. *Gruppe* pilots reportedly to serve with the *Platzschutzstaffel*, was also wounded when he inadvertently taxied over an unexploded bomb buried in the snow at Pitomnik.

Given their longer time at Pitomnik, it was perhaps inevitable that I./JG 3 should sustain the majority of what losses there were. Four of the *Gruppe's* half-dozen or so casualties were aces. Six-victory Unteroffizier Heinrich Blaut of 3. *Staffel* became a PoW after being shot down by a Soviet Yak fighter outside the perimeter on 30 November. 2./JG 3's Leutnant Georg Schentke, whose score was now just ten short of the century, was declared missing over the same area to the northeast

Reportedly the highest scorer of all the *Platzschutzstaffel* Pitomnik volunteers, Feldwebel Kurt Ebener of 4./JG 3 was credited with no fewer than 33 Soviet aircraft over and around Stalingrad in the space of less than a month. The last four – a pair each of DB-3 bombers and LaGG-3 fighters claimed on 15 January 1943 – took his total to 52, making him a semi-centurion and winning him the Knight's Cross into the bargain. Like Walter Ohlrogge he too was subsequently commissioned and is seen here as a leutnant while serving as an instructor with the JGr Ost

But the *Platzschutzstaffel* also suffered its losses – and none more grievous perhaps than 90-victory Leutnant Georg Schentke of 2./JG 3 (pictured here, left, as an oberfeldwebel with 9. *Staffel*), who was forced to bail out over enemy territory while attacking a formation of Soviet bombers to the northeast of the Stalingrad perimeter on Christmas Day 1942

of the pocket on 25 December. Hit while attacking a formation of bombers, he was last seen descending by parachute. Finally, Unteroffiziere Kurt Hofrath and Heinz Obst (21 and 5 victories, respectively) were both brought down by enemy fire on 3 January 1943 shortly after taking off from Pitomnik at the end of their latest stint of duty with the *Platzschutzstaffel*.

Whether by accident or design, the last ten days of December 1942 had also seen another batch of decorations awarded to members of JG 3. In addition to Ludwig Häfner's posthumous Knight's Cross, II. *Gruppe's* seemingly inseparable Leutnant Rudolf Kirschner and Feldwebel Leopold Münster, and Feldwebel Helmut Rüffler of I./JG 3 – recent semi-centurions all – had also received Knight's Crosses. And on 23 December *Geschwaderkommodore* Major Wolf-Dietrich Wilcke, who had continued to rack up his score to even greater heights since being awarded the Oak Leaves for his century back in September, was presented with the Swords for a total now standing at 155.

However, personal achievements alone could not avert the unfolding tragedy of Stalingrad, which was about to enter its final phase. On 14 January 1943 the last of the Pitomnik volunteers was lost when 3./JG 3's Unteroffizier Richard Eisele was killed in a dogfight almost directly above the field. His 'Black 12' smashed into the ground at its western edge, not far from the *Staffel's* dispersal. Seventy-two hours later the unit's unserviceable fighters were blown up where they stood and their pilots flown out to rejoin their *Gruppen*. The *Platzschutzstaffel* was no more. For some the real suffering was only just beginning. The pilots had been the lucky ones. At least 100 members of JG 3's staff and groundcrew had had to be left behind. After *Generalfeldmarschall* Friedrich Paulus' surrender to Chuikov on 2 February 1943, they accompanied the 250,000 survivors of 6. *Armee* on their march eastwards into long years of Soviet captivity. Few, if any, would return home after the war.

By the time the *Platzschutzstaffel* was disbanded, the Red Army had already advanced well beyond Stalingrad. In the face of this threat JG 3's *Gruppen* had been forced to vacate Morosovskaya and retire further west to fields behind the River Donetz. It was from here, at the end of January 1943, that I./JG 3 was withdrawn from the Russian front altogether and transferred back to Germany to prepare for Defence of the Reich duties.

Meanwhile, II. and III. *Gruppen* would soldier on in the east. Compared to the traumatic months leading up to the German defeat at Stalingrad, February to June 1943 remained relatively quiet as both sides sought to build up their strength for the next major confrontation. But 'quiet' should not be confused with uneventful. All along the front a series of local spring offensives by the Soviets would continue to exert enormous pressure on the Germans and their Axis allies. Nowhere was this more evident than on the southern sector – the domain of JG 3 – where the Red Army had recaptured Rostov-on-Don on 14 February and was now attempting a thrust into the Ukraine, which was aimed at cutting off those German forces that had earlier advanced down into the Caucasus.

Geschwaderkommodore Major Wolf-Dietrich Wilcke – seen here (right) in the company of Major Wolfgang Ewald, the *Kommandeur* of III. *Gruppe* – was the third serving member of JG 3 to be awarded the Swords (on 28 December 1942 for 155 victories)

II. and III./JG 3 would become heavily involved in defending the southern Ukraine and protecting the Kuban bridgehead, 17. *Armee's* major escape route out of the Caucasus. In the five months from February to June 1943, the two *Gruppen* would be credited with the destruction of more than 850 enemy aircraft, with II./JG 3 being responsible for well over two-thirds of that total.

During this time II. *Gruppe* lost three of its promising new aces, all with scores close to 20, but welcomed the addition of 18 new ones to its ranks. Times were changing, however, and five victories were no longer an automatic springboard to bigger and better things. The Red Air Force was now stronger, its aircrews being experienced and much better led. A pilot who achieved five kills at this stage of the war needed luck, as well as skill, to progress into double figures. There were a fortunate few who had both in abundance.

Two of the *Gruppe's* 18 new aces of this period would go on to achieve considerable success. 4./JG 3's Leutnant Franz Ruhl, whose fifth had been a LaGG-3 claimed on 28 April, would have earned the Knight's Cross before being killed in action late in 1944. And Unteroffizier Gerhard Thyben of 6. *Staffel*, who had also reached acedom by despatching a LaGG-3 (downed on 11 May), would prove to be one of the most successful of all the mid-war generation of younger fighter pilots. By its end he was serving with JG 54, was wearing the Oak Leaves and had amassed 157 victories.

But it was the *Gruppe's* 'old guard', a handful of highly experienced *Experten*, who continued to take the greatest toll of the enemy. The latter half of March 1943 saw Leutnant Wolf Ettel of 4./JG 3 and Feldwebel August Dilling of 5./JG 3 both join the ranks of the semi-centurions, while on the very last day of the month Dilling's *Staffelkapitän*, Oberleutnant Joachim Kirschner, raised his total to 70 with the first of a trio of Lavochkin fighters.

20 April 1943 was one of II./JG 3's busiest days over the Kuban bridgehead. By its close the *Gruppe* had been credited with 32 enemy aircraft destroyed. Two among that number had provided the 60th for Feldwebel Leopold Münster of 4. *Staffel* and given Joachim Kirschner his 19th. The day also witnessed Major Kurt Brändle's return to ops after two months' absence. A LaGG-3 and an Il-2 claimed within seconds of each other took the *Gruppenkommandeur's* total to 132. And before the month was out two new centurions had emerged. Joachim Kirschner's 100th was a Boston – probably of the Soviet Black Sea Fleet's naval air arm – downed on 27 April. Leutnant Wolf Ettel reached triple figures 24 hours later with the last of a quartet of LaGG-3s.

By 11 May Wolf Ettel's score had risen to 120. This won him the Knight's Cross on 1 June. Four days later he was appointed *Staffelkapitän* of 8./JG 27 in southern Greece. He would add four more enemy aircraft to his overall total – two Spitfires and a pair of B-24 Liberators – before taking a direct hit from Allied anti-aircraft fire whilst on a low-level sweep over Sicily on 17 July 1943.

During this first half of 1943 III./JG 3's experiences had been very similar to those of II. *Gruppe*, albeit on a somewhat smaller scale. Between late March and early May III./JG 3 produced just four new five-victory aces. Against this it suffered the loss of two (including one of the above

In the aftermath of Stalingrad 88-victory Leutnant Eberhard von Boremski of 7./JG 3 was seconded to serve as a fighter instructor with the Rumanian Air Force. He is shown here (second right) with pilots of a Rumanian Bf 109 squadron

foursome). The unit did, however, welcome three new semi-centurions into its ranks. The first was 7. *Staffel's* Oberfeldwebel Hans Schleef, who had claimed his 50th on 2 March. He was followed by Oberleutnant Emil Bitsch of 8./JG 3, whose Il-2 of 19 March provided him with his half-century. Lastly came Feldwebel Hans Reiff, also of 8. *Staffel*. He was responsible for the only two successes credited to the *Gruppe* on 15 April – an I-153 and a Pe-2. They were victories Nos 50 and 51 for Feldwebel Reiff.

III./JG 3 boasted a pair of even higher scoring *Experten* at this time, both of whom were *Staffelkapitäne*. Leutnant Wilhelm Lemke of 9./JG 3 had claimed his century with an La-5 shot down on 16 March. And just over two weeks later, on 1 April, a MiG-3 had been the 80th for Oberleutnant Franz Beyer of 8./JG 3. Shortly thereafter the now Hauptmann Franz Beyer was ordered back to Neubiberg, outside Munich, to become the first *Gruppenkommandeur* of the newly forming IV./JG 3.

Then, on 5 July 1943, the long-awaited blow finally fell. Hitler launched his Operation *Zitadelle*, designed to pinch off and eliminate a dangerous Soviet salient thrusting deep into the German front to the west of Kursk. *Zitadelle* is now famous for developing into the largest tank battle in military history. It also gave JG 3 its most successful day of the entire war.

The War Diary of the German Armed Forces High Command stated, 'Early on 5 July, Operation *Zitadelle* commenced according to plan'. III./JG 3's war diary was much more specific, logging the first of the day's aerial victories to 8. *Staffel's* Leutnant Erwin Stahlberg at 0321 hrs. By its close at around 1900 hrs the pilots of II. and III./JG 3 would, between them, have amassed a staggering 121(!) Soviet aircraft shot down.

With the *Geschwaderstab* having returned to the Reich back in April, the two *Gruppen* were operating under the temporary command of JG 52 when they took up station on two fields along the southern flank of the Kursk salient. The incredible number of successes they claimed on 5 July – the vast majority of them Il-2 *Shturmoviks* and Pe-2 attack bombers – included fifth victories for no fewer than seven brand new aces. The day also witnessed the loss of two existing aces. Both were members of III./JG 3 and both forced-landed behind enemy lines. Unteroffizier Heinz Lüdtke, who had claimed his fifth kill back on 6 May and had added just two more since, ended up in Soviet captivity, while 36-victory Feldwebel Emil Zibler, who was seen to belly-land north of Belgorod after attacking a gaggle of Pe-2s, was posted missing.

At the other end of the scoreboard spectrum II./JG 3's two foremost *Experten* both reached the 150 mark on this 5 July. *Gruppenkommandeur* Major Kurt Brändle and Oberleutnant Joachim Kirschner, the *Kapitän* of 5. *Staffel*, started the day with totals of 146 and 148, respectively. Before darkness fell Joachim Kirschner had accounted for eight(!) Il-2s and a single Yak-1. Kurt Brändle's bag for the day had been a more modest four Il-2s and a single Yak-1. Kirschner's 150th (the second of his eight Ilyushins) went down shortly after 0330 hrs. Very nearly seven more hours would pass before the third of the *Gruppenkommandeur's* four Il-2s took him to 150.

The *Geschwader* was never able to repeat its success of 5 July 1943. Only twice during the remainder of that month did II. *Gruppe* manage to take its collective daily total above 20 – III./JG 3 did not exceed 16. Between them, however, the two *Gruppen did* produce seven more five-victory aces and, on 21 July, a brand new centurion each. Oberleutnant Werner Lucas, who had been appointed *Staffelkapitän* of 4./JG 3 back in November 1942 as the battle for Stalingrad was nearing its climax, downed an Il-2 to obtain his 100. Oberleutnant Emil Bitsch, who had taken over 8. *Staffel* on 1 June 1943 after the departure of Franz Beyer, reached triple figures by despatching an La-5. And on that same 21 July, 7. *Staffel's* long-serving Oberfeldwebel Hans Schleef got his 90th.

On the debit side the two *Gruppen* lost another five aces, including Major Wolfgang Ewald, who had been in command of III./JG 3 since July 1942. On 14 July 1943 the 73-victory Major Ewald had to take to his parachute when his machine was hit by flak northeast of Belgorod. Coming down behind enemy lines, Ewald would endure many years as a prisoner of the Soviets.

In the early evening of 1 August 1943 recent semi-centurion Feldwebel Hans Grünberg of 5./JG 3 claimed his 61st victory. Fittingly perhaps, it was yet another Il-2 *Shturmovik* – arguably JG 3's most formidable opponent in the east – for Grünberg's victim was also the last enemy machine to be downed by the *Geschwader* over Russia. Within hours of its demise II. and III./JG 3 were en route back to the Reich. There they would find themselves facing an entirely new adversary and fighting an entirely new kind of war.

Jagdgeschwader 3's highest scorer of all, Oberleutnant Joachim Kirschner (the *Kapitän* of 5. *Staffel*) is seen here in the summer of 1943 immediately prior to the award of the Oak Leaves on 2 August for his then total of 170 victories. He would subsequently add just five more in early Defence of the Reich operations before being appointed *Gruppenkommandeur* of IV./JG 27 in October

Feldwebel Hans Grünberg, one of the experienced NCO pilots of Oberleutnant Kirschner's 5. *Staffel*, was credited with the very last of the more than 5000 Soviet Air Force machines that fell to the guns of *Jagdgeschwader* 3 in Russia

COLOUR PLATES

1
Bf 109E-4 'Black Chevron and Triangle' of Hauptmann Günther Lützow, *Gruppenkommandeur* I./JG 3, Hargimont, Belgium, May 1940

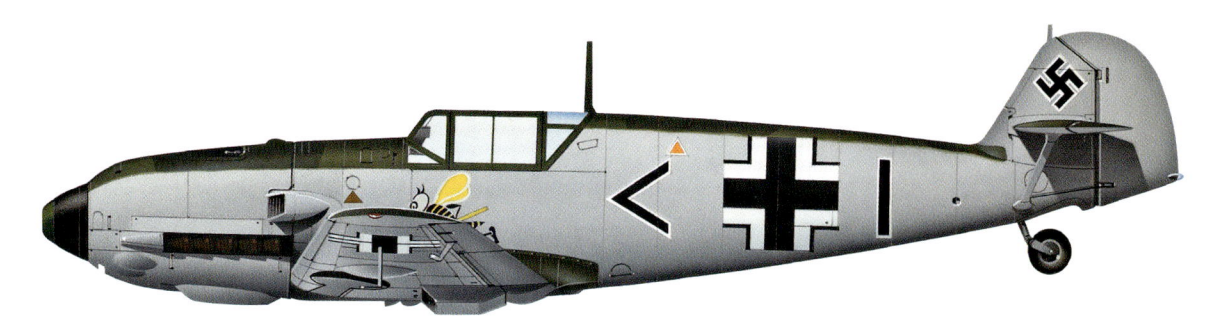

2
Bf 109E-4 'Black Chevron' of Leutnant Egon Troha, *Gruppen*-Adjutant III./JG 3, St Trond, Belgium, May 1940

3
Bf 109E-4 'Black Chevron and Triangle' of Hauptmann Günther Lützow, *Gruppenkommandeur* I./JG 3, Berneuil, France, June 1940

4
Bf 109E-1 'Black 5' of Leutnant Franz Beyer, 8./JG 3, Desvres, France, September 1940

5
Bf 109E-4 'Black Chevron and Circle' of Leutnant Detlev Rohwer, *Gruppen-TO* I./JG 3, Colombert, France, September 1940

6
Bf 109E-4 'Black 1' of Oberleutnant Herbert Kijewski, *Staffelkapitän* 5./JG 3, Wierre-au-Bois, France, September 1940

7
Bf 109E-4 'Black 6' of Unteroffizier Alfred Heckmann, 5./JG 3, Arques, France, September 1940

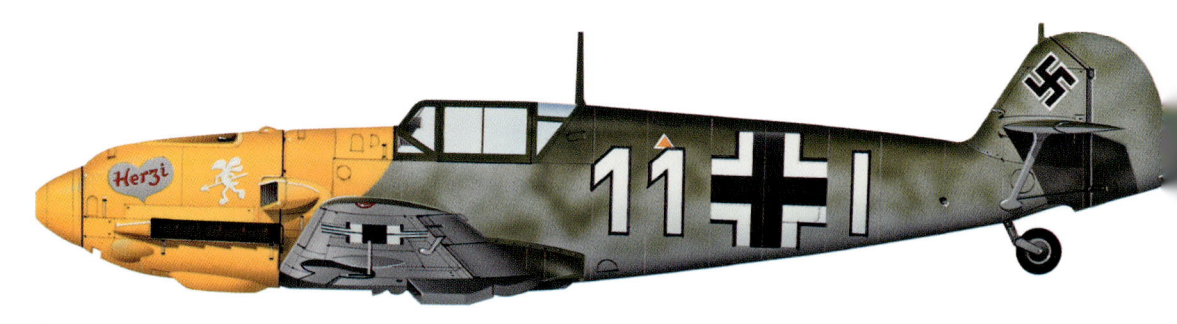

8
Bf 109E-4 'White 11' of Leutnant Alfons Raich, 7./JG 3, Desvres, France, September 1940

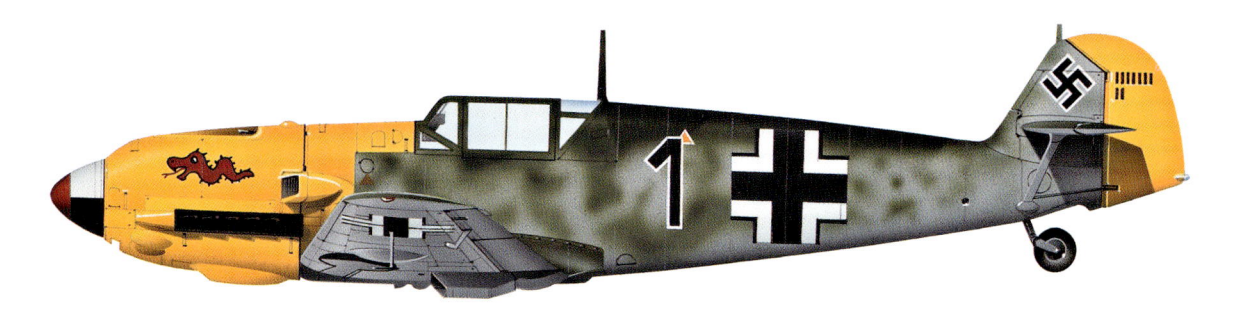

9
Bf 109E-7 'Black 1' of Leutnant Helmut Meckel, *Staffelkapitän* 2./JG 3, St Omer-Wizernes, France, October 1940

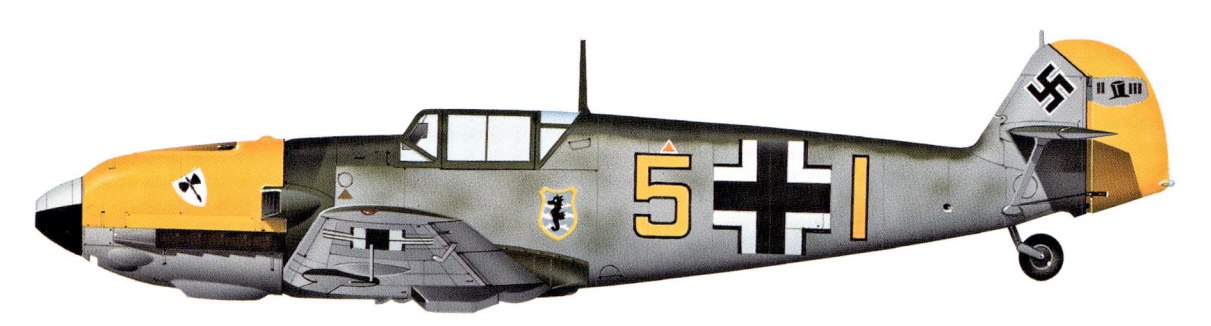

10
Bf 109E-4 'Yellow 5' of Oberleutnant Egon Troha, *Staffelkapitän* 9./JG 3, Desvres, France, October 1940

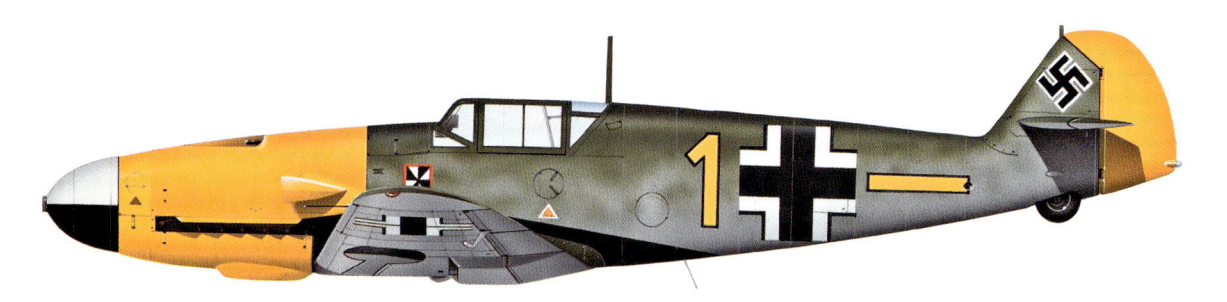

11
Bf 109F-2 'Yellow 1' of Oberleutnant Heinrich Sannemann, *Staffelkapitän* 6./JG 3, Monchy-Breton, France, May 1941

12
Bf 109F-2 'White 7' of Oberleutnant Robert Olejnik, *Staffelkapitän* 1./JG 3, Luzk, Poland, July 1941

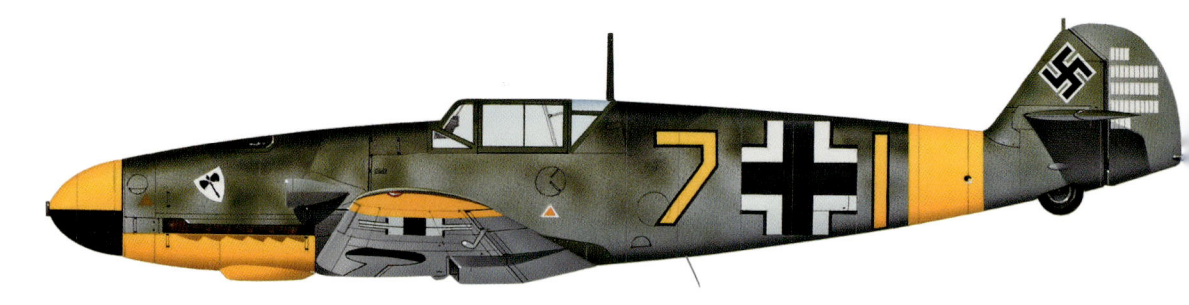

13
Bf 109F-2 'Yellow 7' of Oberleutnant Viktor Bauer, *Staffelkapitän* 9./JG 3, Polonoye, USSR, July 1941

14
Bf 109F-2 'Yellow 6' of Leutnant Helmut Mertens, 9./JG 3, Belaya-Zerkov, USSR, August 1941

15
Bf 109F-4 'Black Chevron and Triangle' of Hauptmann Gordon M Gollob, *Gruppenkommandeur* II./JG 3, Mironovka, USSR, September 1941

16
Bf 109F-4/trop 'Black Chevron and Bar' of Leutnant Max-Bruno Fischer, *Gruppen*-Adjutant II./JG 3 'Udet', Sciacca, Sicily, February 1942

17
Bf 109F-4/Z 'Yellow 4' of Oberfeldwebel Eberhard von Boremski, 9./JG 3 'Udet', Soltsy, USSR, February 1942

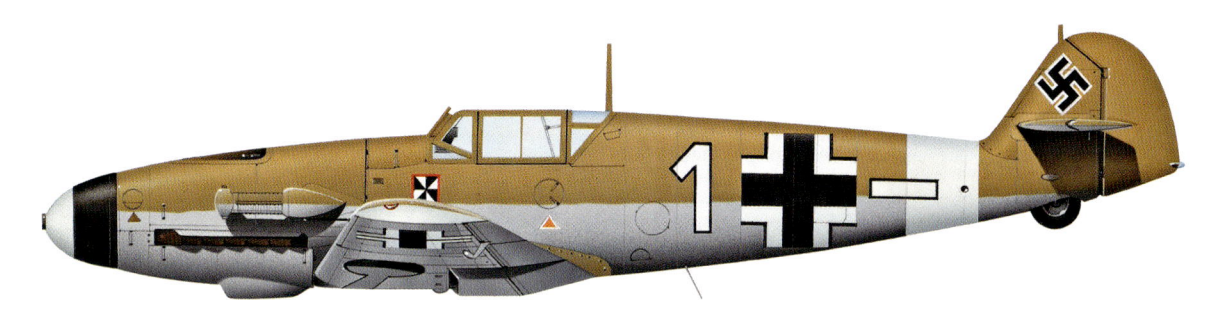

18
Bf 109F-4/trop 'White 1' of Oberleutnant Walther Dahl, *Staffelkapitän* 4./JG 3 'Udet', San Pietro, Sicily, March 1942

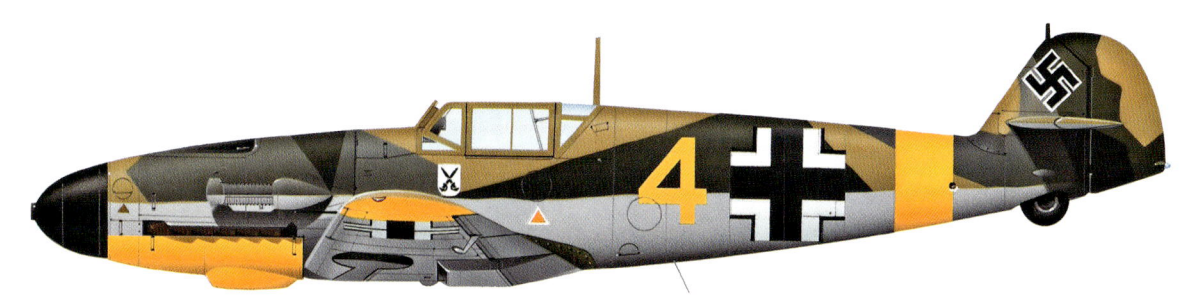

19
Bf 109F-4/trop 'Yellow 4' of Obergefreiter Walther Hagenah, 3./JG 3 'Udet', Wiesbaden-Erbenheim, Germany, April 1942

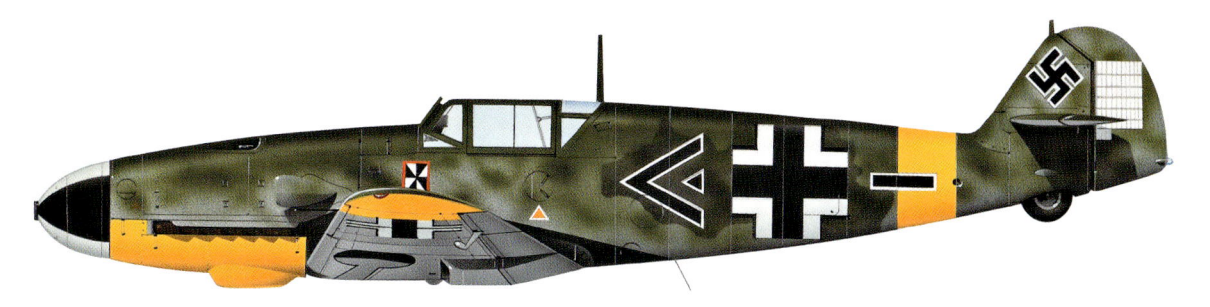

20
Bf 109F-4/trop 'Black Chevron and Triangle' of Hauptmann Kurt Brändle, *Gruppenkommandeur* II./JG 3 'Udet', Mariyevka, USSR, July 1942

21
Bf 109F-4 'Black Chevron and Circle' of Leutnant Heinrich *Graf* von Einsiedel, *Gruppen*-Adjutant III./JG 3 'Udet', Millerovo, USSR, July 1942

22
Bf 109G-2 'Black Chevron and Bars' of Major Wolf-Dietrich Wilcke, *Geschwaderkommodore* JG 3 'Udet', Morosovskaya-West, USSR, December 1942

23
Bf 109G-2 'Black 1' of Leutnant Joachim Kirschner, *Staffelkapitän* 5./JG 3 'Udet', Morosovskaya-South, USSR, December 1942

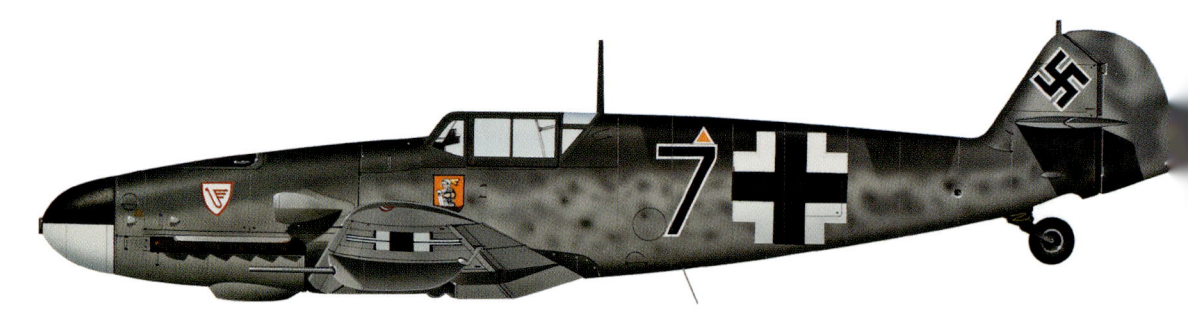

24
Bf 109G-4 'Black 7' of Oberleutnant Detlev Rohwer, *Staffelkapitän* 2./JG 3 'Udet', Mönchen-Gladbach, Germany, May 1943

25
Bf 109G-6/trop 'Black 11' of Feldwebel Hans Kühnel, 11./JG 3 'Udet', San Severo, Italy, August 1943

26
Bf 109G-6y 'Yellow 6' of Oberfeldwebel Alfred Surau, 9./JG 3 'Udet', Bad Wörishofen, Germany, September 1943

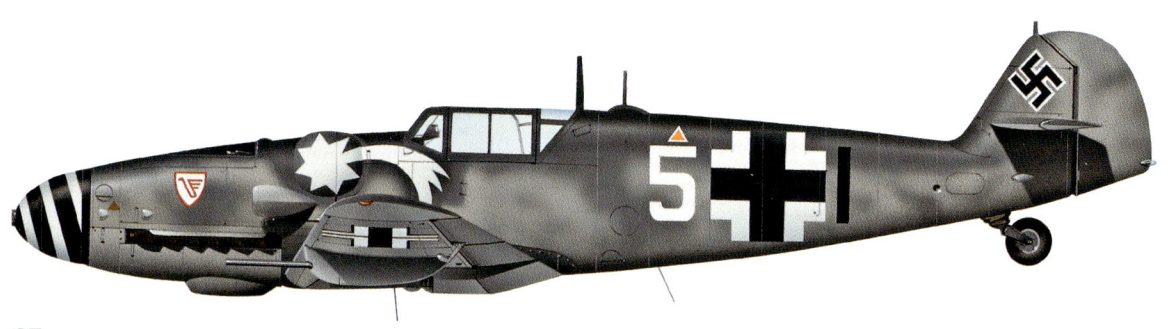

27
Bf 109G-6y 'White 5' of Leutnant Erwin Stahlberg, acting-*Staffelkapitän* 7./JG 3 'Udet', Bad Wörishofen, Germany, October 1943

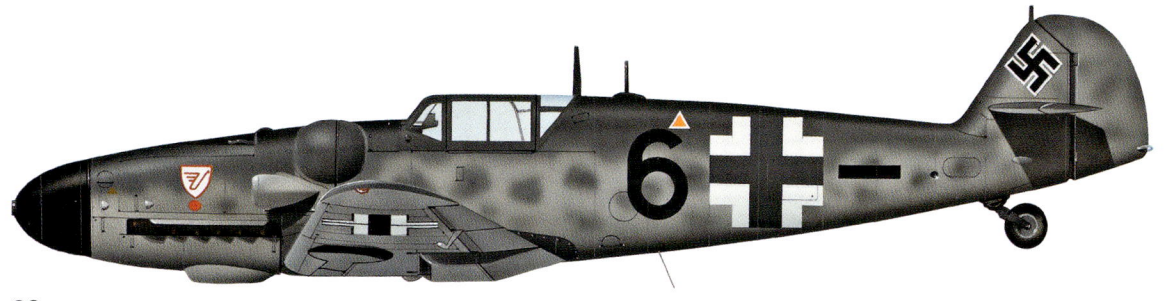

28
Bf 109G-5 'Black 6' of Leutnant Walter Bohatsch, 5./JG 3 'Udet', Schiphol, the Netherlands, November 1943

29
Bf 109G-6/AS 'Black 7' of Leutnant Walter Bohatsch, acting-*Staffelkapitän* 2./JG 3 'Udet', Burg bei Magdeburg, Germany, May 1944

30
Fw 190A-8/R-2 'Black 14' of Unteroffizier Oskar Bösch, 14.(*Sturm*)/JG 3 'Udet', Schafstädt, Germany, October 1944

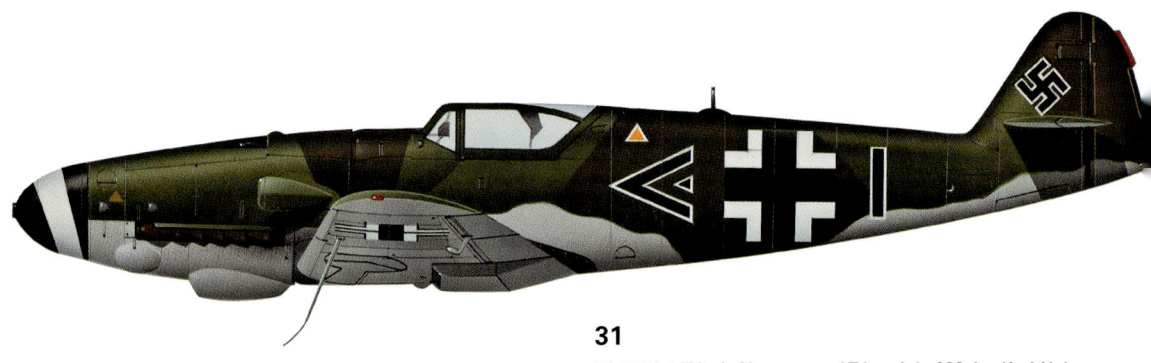

31
Bf 109K-4 'Black Chevron and Triangle' of Major Karl-Heinz Langer, *Gruppenkommandeur* III./JG 3 'Udet', Pasewalk, Germany, April 1945

32
Fw 190D-9 'Green 7' of Feldwebel Hubert Drdla, 13.(*Sturm*)/JG 3 'Udet', Prenzlau, Germany, April 1945

DEFENCE OF THE REICH

Hauptmann Klaus Quaet-Faslem's I./JG 3, the first of the *Geschwader's Gruppen* to be committed to the defence of the Reich, had already experienced just *how* different – and how hard – the air war in the west was going to be. Having been withdrawn from the eastern front towards the end of the battle for Stalingrad, I./JG 3 had spent many months resting and retraining for its new role. The unit returned to operations in the early summer of 1943 and claimed its first successes – a trio of B-17s – on 22 June (two years to the day, coincidentally, since the launch of *Barbarossa*).

During its first seven weeks in combat the *Gruppe* accounted for just nine B-17s and a single P-38 fighter. These successes had cost the unit a dozen of its own machines destroyed or written off, and four pilots killed – a very far cry from the victory-to-loss ratio it had become accustomed to on the eastern front. Of even more significance, perhaps, was the fact that six of these successes had been 'firsts' for young and inexperienced pilots, not one of whom would go on to achieve five victories against the ever growing might of the USAAF's Eighth Air Force.

This was a recurring theme throughout JG 3's initial year of operations in defence of the Reich. A substantial percentage of its successes would be first kills for younger pilots, the majority of whom would then be able to claim perhaps only one or two more victories before they themselves fell victim to enemy action. There were, of course, the proven veterans of the eastern front, many – but by no means all – of whom would return to the Reich to continue adding to their already considerable scores. But the rate of increase was much slower. Multiple daily victories were now a thing of the past. For a pilot to achieve more than one kill on any one day in the skies above Germany would quickly become the exception rather than the rule. And the casualties among the ranks of these veterans also began to mount as the American daylight bombing offensive grew in strength.

The losses in experienced formation leaders were of particular concern. In the year ahead JG 3 would lose no fewer than two *Geschwaderkommodores*, six *Gruppenkommandeure* and 14 *Staffelkapitäne*!

In August 1943 another of JG 3's *Gruppen* was added to the Defence of the Reich order of battle. Unlike I./JG 3, however, III. *Gruppe* – under its new *Kommandeur*, Hauptmann Walther Dahl – had been denied the benefit of a lengthy period of retraining. In fact, the unit was transferred from east to west with almost indecent haste. On the morning of 1 August 1943 III./JG 3 had been credited with its final four kills over Russia. One of them, a Yak fighter, had given 7. *Staffel's* Oberfeldwebel Hans Schleef victory No 94. Just 12 days later the same Hans Schleef opened the *Gruppe's* Defence of the Reich scoreboard by claiming his 95th – the first of three B-17s brought down northeast of Cologne.

The hasty recall to the homeland had clearly had no ill effects on III./JG 3. Quite the reverse, it would seem, for Hauptmann Dahl's *Gruppe* would emerge from this first round of operations in defence of the Reich as the most successful of the three *Gruppen* both in terms of victories gained and casualties suffered. By the end of May 1944 III./JG 3 would have added 185 US aircraft – the overwhelming majority of them four-engined bombers – to its collective scoreboard for the loss of 'only' 44 of its own pilots killed (plus a further 27 wounded or injured). During this period it also produced the highest number of new five-victory aces – nine in all – as opposed to I. and II. *Gruppen's* four apiece.

At the other end of the scale III. *Gruppe's* small band of *'alte Hasen'* ('old hares', the Luftwaffe's term for combat-savvy veterans) were also adding to their scores. But they were not finding it as easy as it had been in Russia. Every single victory against the Americans had to be hard fought for.

It was one of the 'old hares', Hauptmann Wilhelm Lemke, *Kapitän* of 9. *Staffel*, who was responsible for two of the four kills credited to the *Gruppe* on its second Defence of the Reich mission. 17 August 1943 was the day that the 'Mighty Eighth' staged its ill-fated double strike against Schweinfurt and Regensburg. Lemke's pair of P-47 Thunderbolts took his overall total to 127. I./JG 3 was also in action on this date, claiming a creditable six B-17s without loss. Two of the Fortresses provided victories No 48 for *Gruppenkommandeur* Hauptmann Klaus Quaet-Faslem and No 53 for Oberleutnant Helmut Mertens, the *Kapitän* of his 1. *Staffel*.

JG 3's only successes the following month were the 11 B-17s brought down during the 6 September raid on Stuttgart (described by one historian as 'one of the most costly fiascos in Eighth Air Force history'). All but one of these victories were credited to pilots of III./JG 3, with the 'old hares' again featuring prominently. Adding to their scores were *Kommandeur* Hauptmann Walther Dahl (Nos 52 and 53), Hauptmann Wilhelm Lemke (128), Leutnant Hans Schleef (96) and 9. *Staffel's* Oberfeldwebel Alfred Surau (42 and 43). The 11th Fortress was claimed by the *Geschwader*-Adjutant, Oberleutnant Hermann *Freiherr* von Kap-herr, *Stab* JG 3 having commenced operations over Germany on this very day.

On 12 September JG 3's Defence of the Reich line-up was completed by the arrival of Major Kurt Brändle's II. *Gruppe*. Having been withdrawn from the Russian front early in August, II./JG 3 had spent a month under training in northern Germany before its transfer to Schiphol, in Holland. This placed it very much in the frontline of homeland defence operations, as the *Gruppe's* lengthening casualty lists were soon to prove. The 169 victories it claimed over the next nine months would be achieved at a cost of 82 fighter pilots killed, missing or wounded – among them seven highly experienced formation leaders.

The first two of those 169 enemy aircraft destroyed were a pair of RAF Coastal Command Beaufighters that were part of a force busily attacking German minesweepers off the Dutch coast in the early evening of 16 September. Caught by 4./JG 3, the two Beaufighters were victories Nos 21 and 42 for Leutnant

II./JG 3's first 'Defence of the Reich' victories were, in fact, a brace of RAF Beaufighters that were attacking German minesweepers off the Dutch coast. The first of the pair provided victory No 21 for 4. *Staffel's* Leutnant Franz Ruhl, portrayed here sporting the Knight's Cross awarded to him in July 1944

Franz Ruhl and Fahnenjunker-Feldwebel Hans Frese, respectively. Based so close to the North Sea coast, II./JG 3 was the only *Gruppe* to encounter patrolling RAF aircraft at this time. Before the year was out it would bring down nine more British machines – the only non-American aircraft out of the *Geschwader's* collective total of 700+ claims for the 12 months from June 1943 to May 1944.

On 24 September Hauptmann Joachim Kirschner, the *Kapitän* of 5. *Staffel*, who had been awarded the Oak Leaves (for his 170 victories) on the day that II./JG 3 had left Russia, downed the *Gruppe's* first B-17 in the west. This was the start of the steady, if unspectacular, toll of US bombers and their escorting fighters that the *Gruppe* would continue to claim in the months ahead. But it was their grievous losses that overshadowed the last quarter of 1943.

Among the 23 pilots killed or missing were the first of the experienced, high-scoring unit leaders. On 18 October (the day that 175-victory Hauptmann Joachim Kirschner departed to take command of IV./JG 27 in Greece) another of the *Gruppe's* long-serving *Staffelkapitäne*, Hauptmann Paul Stolte of 6./JG 3, was reported missing. A heavy blanket of fog had suddenly descended over the Dutch coast on that date, and it was presumed that Stolte had gone down into the North Sea.

On 24 September 1943, eight days after the Beaufighters went down, Hauptmann Joachim Kirschner claimed his first Defence of the Reich kill and II. *Gruppe's* first four-engined bomber – a Fortress of the USAAF's 100th BG reportedly engaged on a practice Pathfinder Force mission over the North Sea. Three more B-17s and a Spitfire would complete his tally with JG 3 before his posting to the Mediterranean on 18 October

Just six days later yet another *Staffelkapitän*, Oberleutnant Werner Lucas of 4./JG 3, who had claimed a single Fortress since arriving in Holland to take his overall score to 106, was killed in a dogfight with RAF Spitfires to the southwest of Amsterdam. Nor was that all. At around midday on 3 November *Gruppenkommandeur* Major Kurt Brändle had accounted for a pair of P-47s, part of the fighter escort for a heavy Fortress raid on Wilhelmshaven. His first victories in defence of the Reich, the two Thunderbolts had raised Brändle's total to 172 – but they were also to be his last.

II./JG 3 had returned to Schiphol when, later that same afternoon, the field was attacked by a force of twin-engined B-26 Marauders. The *Gruppe* scrambled as the first bombs were falling and chased the intruders back out to sea, only to fall foul of their escorting Spitfires. Five pilots were killed in the ensuing dogfight, including Major Kurt Brändle, whose body was washed ashore more than two months later.

Brändle's successor at the head of the *Gruppe* was not to survive for long either. During his brief tenure of office Hauptmann Wilhelm Lemke, previously the *Kapitän* of 9./JG 3, had received the Oak Leaves on 25 November for a score then standing at 130. He would add just one more while *Kommandeur* of II. *Gruppe* – a P-47 claimed on 30 November – before he was himself shot down by Thunderbolts west of Nijmegen four days later. The loss of two *Gruppenkommandeure* and three *Staffelkapitäne* (one posted away) in the space of less than seven weeks had hit II./JG 3 hard. The *Gruppe's* four leading *Experten* were gone, and they would prove to be impossible to replace as the carnage continued into 1944. Between now and the end of the war only one other centurion would serve within the ranks of II./JG 3, and he came in from another unit with 129 victories already under his belt. He would claim just three more while a member of the *Gruppe*.

Meanwhile, the other two *Gruppen* back in Germany – I./JG 3 at Bönninghardt and III./JG 3 at Bad Wörishofen – had suffered far less attrition in the closing months of 1943. Unlike II./JG 3 up on the Dutch coast, they did not have to face almost daily incursions by enemy aircraft. In fact, weeks would go by without their claiming a single kill.

I./JG 3, for example, added just 11 US bombers and fighters to its unit scoreboard between mid-August and the end of 1943. After Leutnant Franz Schwaiger's single Fortress of 19 August (his 56th victory to date), September would see no successes whatsoever and October just three. These three were all credited to the *Kapitän* of 2. *Staffel*, Hauptmann Detlev Rohwer. The second of them, which took Rohwer's tally to 32, was a P-47 downed on 14 October. This was the day the 'Mighty Eighth' made its second trip to Schweinfurt. The early confrontation with a pack of escorting fighters over Antwerp, in Belgium, had cost I. *Gruppe* three pilots killed, among them seven-victory Hauptmann Rudolf Germeroth, the *Staffelkapitän* of 3./JG 3.

Later, as the US bombers neared Frankfurt, they were set upon by Hauptmann Walther Dahl's III./JG 3, which claimed 18 Fortresses for the loss of one of its own number. The victorious pilots included both *Experte* and tyro alike. The *Gruppenkommandeur* was credited with two of the B-17s (Nos 54 and 55), as was the *Kapitän* of 9. *Staffel*, Hauptmann Wilhelm Lemke (these were Nos 129 and 130 for Lemke, and his last before being appointed *Kommandeur* of II./JG 3 in place of the missing Kurt Brändle). Fellow *Staffelkapitän* and recent Knight's Cross recipient Oberleutnant Emil Bitsch of 8./JG 3 got his 106th. Among the tyros, there was a fifth for Leutnant Jürgen Hoerschelmann and firsts for future aces Unteroffizier Gerhard Pankalla and Feldwebel Paul Wielebinski.

Hauptmann Walther Dahl, now the *Kommandeur* of III. *Gruppe*, congratulates three NCOs of his 7. *Staffel* after the *Gruppe's* successful action against the Eighth Air Force during 'second Schweinfurt'. Between them, the four pilots shown here were credited with six of the 18 Fortresses claimed by III./JG 3 on that 14 October. They are, from left, Unteroffizier Gerhard Pankalla (victory No 1), Feldwebel Kurt Gräf (No 12), Unteroffizier Wolfgang Rentsch (Nos 3 and 4), and Hauptmann Dahl himself (Nos 54 and 55)

III./JG 3's sole loss on 14 October 1943 was Oberfeldwebel Alfred Surau of 9. *Staffel*. He is pictured here, right, sitting on the wing of a machine that is clearly not the 'Yellow 6' (see colour profile 26) from which he was to bail out fatally wounded some 60 kilometres to the southwest of Schweinfurt after claiming his 46th, and final, victory

The *Gruppe's* sole fatality was 46-victory Oberfeldwebel Alfred Surau, currently the unit's highest scoring NCO pilot and a true 'old hare'. Hit by return fire from the B-17 he was attacking, Surau was severely wounded. Although he managed to take to his parachute, he succumbed to his injuries before the day was out.

III./JG 3 did not see action again until 19 December, when it knocked eight Fortresses out of a Fifteenth Air Force formation flying up from Italy to attack the Messerschmitt aircraft plant at Augsburg.

Having been transferred to Vendeville, in northeast France, I. *Gruppe's* total bag for December was just four US fighters. They had provided firsts for each of the four young NCO pilots involved, only one of whom subsequently went on to become an ace. And it would take Unteroffizier Hans Fritz of 3. *Staffel* just four days short of a full year to add another 11 victories to the P-38 Lightning that he had downed on 1 December 1943 before he was himself lost in action on 26 November 1944. This was another graphic example of the huge difference between western and eastern fronts, where a dozen kills could be – and often were – racked up in two or three weeks.

December's other three successes had been a trio of Thunderbolts all brought down on the 30th. And, even more typical of the times, two of the three claimants had themselves failed to survive the engagement, both being promptly shot down by other P-47s close to the Franco-Belgian border.

The most significant event of December 1943, however, was the arrival in Belgium of a fourth *Gruppe*. This unit, IV./JG 3, had been activated at Neubiberg, near Munich, back in June. Formed around a small cadre of experienced pilots from the *Geschwader's* other *Gruppen* and placed under the command of Hauptmann Franz Beyer (ex-*Staffelkapitän* of 8./JG 3), it had initially been deployed to the Mediterranean theatre, where it saw several weeks' action over Sicily and southern Italy, including the defence of the Salerno beachhead.

Between early July and mid-September 1943 the *Gruppe* was credited with 66 enemy aircraft destroyed. The majority were claimed by the 'old hares' drafted in from other units (only two new five-victory aces emerged during this period). And although Hauptmann Beyer managed to add only two more kills to his existing score of 80, his three veteran *Staffelkapitäne* each brought down eight apiece. Leutnant Otto Wessling of 10. *Staffel* (who had earlier served with both I. and III./JG 3) took his

A Bf 109G-6/trop of IV./JG 3 seen at San Severo, northwest of Foggia, Italy, in August 1943. It is purportedly 'Yellow 14', the mount of Leutnant Herbert Kutscha, the *Kapitän* of 12. *Staffel*. An ex-Bf 110 pilot, Herbert Kutscha would claim 12 victories (out of an overall total of 47) while serving with JG 3. Note the 21 cm underwing rocket-launcher tube and the smaller style 'winged U' *Geschwader* badge favoured by IV. *Gruppe*

total from 62 to 70. Oberleutnant Gustav Frielinghaus of 11. *Staffel* (ex-II. *Gruppe*) increased his tally from 66 to 74, and 12. *Staffel's* Oberleutnant Herbert Kutscha, who had previously flown twin-engined Bf 110s on the eastern front, upped his overall score to 32.

IV./JG 3's Mediterranean successes had not come cheaply, however. Its 66 victories against the Anglo-American forces cost the unit 13 pilots killed and 14 wounded or injured. Among the early losses was Oberleutnant Franz Daspelgruber, the first *Staffelkapitän* of 10./JG 3 (and before that a member of 3./JG 3), who managed to claim a single B-24 Liberator on 2 July – thereby taking his total to 46 – before failing to return from a mission over the Gulf of Taranto exactly two weeks later.

Daspelgruber's successor as *Kapitän* of 10. *Staffel*, Leutnant Otto Wessling, was seriously injured in a bombing raid on the *Gruppe's* base at Leverano, on the heel of Italy, on 23 July. Four other pilots were injured and three killed – among the latter, 17-victory Feldwebel Uwe Krais – in this devastating attack delivered by B-17s flying up from North Africa. With more than 60 groundcrew also killed or wounded and some 40 fighters destroyed or severely damaged, it was a blow that effectively ended IV./JG 3's Italian odyssey. Not long afterwards the *Gruppe* was recalled to Neubiberg for a further lengthy period of rest and re-equipment. And it was from here, on Christmas Eve 1943, that it flew to Grimbergen airfield, near Brussels, to commence Defence of the Reich operations.

1944 began on pretty much the same note as 1943 had ended, with JG 3 continuing to exact a steady, if limited, toll of the US bombers and their escorting fighters. But as the Americans grew ever stronger, so the *Geschwader* found it increasingly difficult to score successes against them. The newer pilots, lacking adequate and proper training, were at a particular disadvantage when faced with the overwhelming might of the enemy. In the five months from January to May 1944 the *Geschwader* – although now four *Gruppen* strong – produced fewer than 30 new five-victory aces (half of them from the ranks of IV./JG 3 alone).

Even the more experienced pilots were adding only slowly and intermittently to their personal tallies. Against this the casualty lists were lengthening at an alarming rate, the losses covering the whole spectrum from the newest tyros, through budding aces and 'old hares', right up to the foremost *Experten*. The *Geschwader's* success – or otherwise – was now being measured not in numbers of enemy aircraft brought down, but in casualties suffered. And, once again, it was the experienced unit commanders, leading from the front, who were bearing the brunt.

The catalogue of losses began on 30 January 1944 with a non-combat fatality when Major Klaus Quaet-Faslem, the long serving *Kommandeur* of I. *Gruppe*, crashed in bad weather near Brunswick. Twelve days later, on 11 February, 83-victory

7. *Staffel's* Feldwebel Wolfgang Rentsch (right) pictured at a snowy Leipheim, west of Augsburg, in early March 1944. Despite the smiles, the war was not going well, and Rentsch's experiences in the first half of 1944 were typical. Having been credited with his seventh victory (a B-17) on 24 February, he was himself wounded on 18 March and was not able to claim his eighth – another B-17 – until 29 May. Wounded again during the Normandy campaign, Wolfgang Rentsch ended the war as a leutnant flying Me 262s with JG 7

Major Franz Beyer, *Gruppenkommandeur* of IV./JG 3, was also killed in a crash. This time the weather was not to blame, his machine clipping a tree during a low-level dogfight with Spitfires to the south of Liège, in Belgium.

Among the *Staffelkapitäne* lost in February were two from IV. *Gruppe*, both having gone down during a sprawling fight with a group of about 50 Thunderbolts over Holland on 10 February. Oberleutnant Alfred Humer of 10. *Staffel* had claimed his 21st victory just a week earlier (his first 20 having been achieved with I. *Gruppe*), while 11. *Staffel's* Leutnant Hermann Schmied's total at the time of his demise was six. And on 22 February, the third day of the Americans' 'Big Week' offensive, 36-victory Oberleutnant Ernst-Heinz Löhr, the *Staffelkapitän* of 1./JG 3, fell victim to Thunderbolts escorting US bombers attacking German aircraft plants.

On the credit side, 23 February closed with III./JG 3 having claimed 15 B-24 Liberators, plus five of their P-38 Lightning escorts, as they retired south across the Alps after raiding targets in Austria. This was one of the most successful days enjoyed by the *Geschwader* during the first half of 1944, surpassed only by IV./JG 3 on two occasions later in the spring. Among the claimants on this date was Major Walther Dahl, whose pair of Liberators and single Lightning took his score to 61. Another of the Liberators provided victory No 108 for the *Gruppe's* sole remaining centurion, Hauptmann Emil Bitsch, the *Staffelkapitän* of 8./JG 3.

The *Geschwader's* first Knight's Cross of 1944 was also awarded in February. It went to Hauptmann Gustav Frielinghaus, *Staffelkapitän* of 11./JG 3, who had been severely wounded back on 9 September 1943 (the first day of the Salerno landings in southern Italy) and would not return to combat flying.

If February's casualty figures had been bad, those for March were even worse. The *Geschwader* lost at least eight aces, among them its two highest scorers. On 15 March, with his total still standing at 108, Hauptmann Emil Bitsch was brought down close to the North Sea coast after clashing with the seemingly ever-present Thunderbolts. But it was 23 March that would prove to be the blackest day of all.

Despite the adverse weather, the Eighth Air Force had despatched more than 700 bombers, escorted by close on 850 fighters, to attack targets of opportunity across northwest Germany. Among

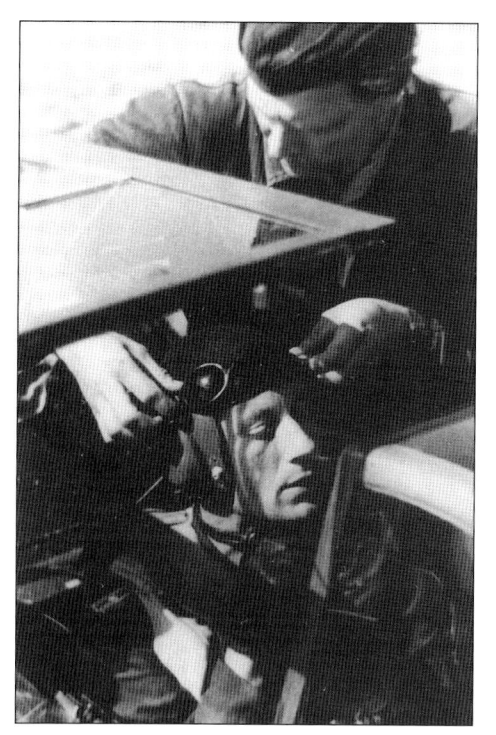

Major Klaus Quaet-Faslem, who had commanded I./JG 3 since August 1942, lost his life when he crashed in bad weather on 30 January 1944. He would be honoured with a posthumous Knight's Cross on 9 June 1944

The first *Geschwaderkommodore* of JG 3 to be killed in action, the then Major Wolf-Dietrich Wilcke had been banned from further combat flying shortly after being awarded the Swords for his 155th victory back in December 1942 (although he had managed to squeeze in one more kill in January 1943). So desperate had the situation become by early 1944, however, that Oberstleutnant Wilcke decided to ignore the ban and resume his leadership of the *Geschwader* in the air. He was able to achieve six victories in Defence of the Reich operations before being shot down by Mustangs on 23 March 1944

the fighters sent up against them were the eight Bf 109Gs of the *Stab* JG 3 led, as usual, by *Kommodore* Oberstleutnant Wolf-Dietrich Wilcke. Since taking command of the *Geschwader* 19 months earlier, Wilcke had exactly doubled his personal score from 80 to 160. Now he was about to add the last two – a B-17 and a P-51 Mustang – before himself finally being brought to bay by P-51s and shot down southeast of Brunswick. In Wilcke the Luftwaffe had lost one of the most highly decorated and successful fighter pilots still flying on operations.

Among the nine other casualties suffered by JG 3 on 23 March were Oberleutnant Hans Schleef, the *Staffelkapitän* of 3./JG 3, who was just two short of his century, and who was seriously injured when his machine somersaulted on landing back at Burg, and 20-victory Feldwebel Rasso Förg of 11./JG 3 who, like his *Kommodore*, also fell victim to Mustangs. Six days later Hauptmann Detlev Rohwer, the *Gruppenkommandeur* of II./JG 3, was forced to land west of Osnabrück after engaging a formation of bombers. He was severely wounded when his machine was then strafed on the ground by P-38 Lightnings. Despite the amputation of one leg, he died the following day.

Nor did the situation improve greatly in April. Despite IV./JG 3 achieving a notable success on 11 April by claiming no fewer than 24 B-17s and a single P-38, the month was again dominated by losses. Among them were two 'old hares' of non-commissioned rank, four *Staffelkapitäne* and yet another *Gruppenkommandeur*.

The first of these was Leutnant Hans-Martin Stein, the *Kapitän* of 9. *Staffel*, who was killed while attempting an emergency landing with a dead engine northwest of Salzburg on 12 April. Three days later 2./JG 3's *Staffelkapitän*, 33-victory Leutnant Harro Schlüter, lost his life in a mid-air collision with a Ju 88 while practising dummy attacks close to I. *Gruppe's* Burg base. Then, on 19 April, IV./JG 3 lost its current top scorer when the *Kapitän* of 11. *Staffel*, Oberleutnant Otto Wessling – who had claimed a trio of B-17s during the action of 11 April to take his score to 80, and had added three more since – suffered a fate similar to that of Detlev Rohwer less than three weeks earlier. After his machine had been damaged in combat to the southwest of Kassel, Wessling put it down in a forced-landing. He was able to escape from the burning fighter, but not from the P-51s that swooped down to strafe it.

On 24 April JG 3 was dealt a double blow. Hauptmann Hermann *Freiherr* von Kap-herr, hitherto the *Geschwader*-Adjutant who had been selected to replace the fallen Detlev Rohwer as *Kommandeur* of II. *Gruppe*, was shot down over Neuburg-on-the-Danube after just two days in office. And Leutnant Franz Schwaiger, the 58-victory *Staffelkapitän* of 1./JG 3, was forced to belly-land in the same area, only to become yet another victim of ground-strafing Mustangs.

For some weeks past a special *Sturmstaffel* of Fw 190s had been operating in conjunction with the Messerschmitts of IV. *Gruppe*. And on 15 April it was announced that IV./JG 3, commanded now by Hauptmann Wilhelm Moritz, had been chosen to become the Luftwaffe's first dedicated *Sturmgruppe*. The unit then spent the remainder of April and much of May converting from its Bf 109Gs onto heavily armed and

And still the losses continued. A month after the *Kommodore* went down, 58-victory Leutnant Franz Schwaiger, the recently-appointed *Staffelkapitän* of 1./JG 3, also fell victim to Mustangs – ground-strafed after successfully belly-landing his damaged 'White 15' on 24 April

armoured Fw 190A-8s (for full details of *Sturm* operations see *Osprey Aviation Elite Units 20 – Luftwaffe Sturmgruppen*).

Meanwhile, the carnage had been continuing among the other *Gruppen*. In the first half of May two more *Staffelkapitäne* went down. 5. *Staffel's* Leutnant Leopold Münster had returned with II. *Gruppe* from the Russian front in August 1943 with 76 victories already to his name. Since that time he had risen to become the *Gruppe's* leading exponent in Defence of the Reich operations. The two bombers he claimed in the Hanover region on 8 May took his overall tally to 95 – the second of them, a B-24 Liberator, was also to be his last. Pressing his attack home too closely, he inadvertently collided with his intended victim, which immediately exploded in mid-air and took Münster's 'Black 1' down with it.

Four days later – on 12 May, the day 'Poldi' Münster was honoured with posthumous Oak Leaves – 7./JG 3 lost its *Staffelkapitän* when 18-victory Leutnant Jürgen Hoerschelmann was shot down in a dogfight with P-51s near Fulda.

Then, on 29 May, JG 3 lost its second *Kommodore* in the space of just over two months. Major Friedrich-Karl Müller had claimed his first victory with JG 53 during the *Blitzkrieg* in the west, and had remained with that *Geschwader* until February 1944 when he was appointed *Gruppenkommandeur* of IV./JG 3. By that time he was wearing the Oak Leaves and had amassed a personal score of 117. Müller added five more – all heavy bombers – during his six weeks in command of IV. *Gruppe* before replacing the fallen Oberstleutnant Wilcke as *Geschwaderkommodore* of JG 3. Flying at the head of the *Geschwader*, Major Müller was to claim a further 18 kills. Again, with but one exception, all were four-engined bombers. But more than four years of near constant frontline service had left their mark. 'Tutti' Müller was by now utterly exhausted both physically and mentally. And it was this combat fatigue which, many of his contemporaries believed, caused him to misjudge his approach and cost him his life when he crashed on landing back at Salzwedel after a mission on 29 May.

It was a tragic ending to another chapter in the *Geschwader's* history. Eight days later, in the early hours of 6 June 1944, Allied forces landed in Normandy.

Among those lost early in May was another *Staffelkapitän* with an even higher score to his credit. Leutnant Leopold Münster of 5./JG 3 claimed his 94th – a B-17 – on the morning of 8 May, but then collided with his next intended victim less than 30 minutes later. The stricken B-24 (possibly of the 445th BG) and 'Poldi' Münster's 'Black 1' both went down west of Goslar

JG 3 lost its second *Kommodore* in the space of little more than two months when, for reasons unknown, 140-victory Major Friedrich-Karl 'Tutti' Müller was forced to abort from the mission he was leading on 29 May 1944. Fatally misjudging his final approach, he crashed on landing back at Salzwedel

NORMANDY BLOODBATH

The Allied landings in Normandy on 6 June 1944 triggered an immediate response from the Luftwaffe. Plans to counter the expected invasion by rushing nearly every Defence of the Reich *Gruppe* to whichever part of the French Channel coast was coming under attack had long been in place. Putting those plans into effect, however, was a different matter entirely. The Allies now enjoyed such absolute air superiority that a mass transfer of units by the Luftwaffe was a hazardous undertaking. Many *Gruppen* suffered severe losses in the attempt, but JG 3 was fortunate in completing the move to France with minimal casualties.

II. and III./JG 3 began arriving at their assigned bases roughly midway between Paris and Caen on 7 June. Over the course of the next 12 weeks the two *Gruppen* would, between them, account for very nearly 100 enemy aircraft destroyed. But the opposition they faced, both in the air and on the ground, was enormous. They would suffer 138 pilot casualties (89 killed or missing) and lose almost 250 aircraft, either shot down or destroyed on the ground by bombing and strafing, plus nearly as many again damaged!

II./JG 3 would prove to be the more successful of the two *Gruppen*. The 51 kills it claimed during the battle of Normandy included eight 'firsts' and produced three new five-victory aces. The *Gruppe's* two highest scorers at this time were Leutnant Hans Grünberg, the *Staffelkapitän* of 5./JG 3, and 4. *Staffel's* Oberfeldwebel Helmut Rüffler. Grünberg was to be credited with seven victories (taking his overall score to 77) before II./JG 3 was

Reportedly the mount of Oberleutnant Max-Bruno Fischer, the *Gruppen*-Adjutant of II./JG 3, this bomb-carrying *Gustav* emerges cautiously from its leafy hide at Evreux during the early days of the Normandy campaign

4. *Staffel's* Oberfeldwebel Helmut Rüffler (second left) claimed four Allied fighters over Normandy. They were to be the last of the 63 victories credited to him as a member of JG 3 before he was himself shot down badly wounded southeast of Caen on 18 July 1944. He would later return to ops with JG 51, taking his final total to 88

pulled out of France at the end of August. Rüffler claimed four – a single Spitfire and three Mustangs. He downed the last two Mustangs, which were also to be the last of his 63 victories with JG 3, during a vicious dogfight near Caen on 18 July, but was then severely wounded himself. Five other pilots were killed in the same action, among them 13-victory Leutnant Robert Roller of 6./JG 3 and 4. *Staffel's* Leutnant Manfred Fedgenhäuer (nine kills).

By contrast, III. *Gruppe's* 47 successes of the Normandy campaign – which cost it 51 pilots killed or missing, plus four shot down and captured – included no fewer than 14 'firsts', yet produced only one (very short-lived) five-victory ace. The two pilots currently heading III./JG 3's scoreboard arrived in France with just 20 and 19 victories, respectively. Oberleutnant Raimund Koch, the *Kapitän* of 8. *Staffel*, claimed his 21st – a P-51 – within hours of touching down at St André. He would add four more US fighters and a single B-17, thereby raising his tally to 26, by the time the *Gruppe* returned to Germany. Hauptmann Karl-Heinz Langer, with 19 victories to his name, had been the *Kapitän* of 7. *Staffel* until he was appointed *Gruppenkommandeur* of III./JG 3 on 21 May after Major Walther Dahl's departure to assume command of JG 300. Langer opened his Normandy scoring with a P-47 and a P-51, both downed on 21 June, before then claiming a P-38 in July and another P-47 in August.

Against these successes, meagre enough as they were, III. *Gruppe* lost a number of aces. And among them was its newest ace of all. The first of the pair of Mustangs that 7. *Staffel's* Feldwebel Paul Wielebinski had claimed on 21 June had given him his fifth victory. Four days later Wielebinski died in hospital after parachuting wounded from his 'Blue 6' during a dogfight southwest of Evreux. And on 11 July Leutnant Dieter Zink, who had recently been transferred in from the *Geschwaderstab* to take command of 9. *Staffel*, parachuted into British captivity after his 'Yellow 13' was damaged by flak near Caen.

It was during July that the Luftwaffe took the decision to strengthen its fighter presence in Normandy by adding a fourth *Staffel* to many of the *Gruppen* struggling to contain the Allied invasion forces. Most, if not all, of these *Staffeln* were culled from units operating on the eastern front. In the case of II. and III./JG 3, the *Staffeln* involved were 4. and 7./JG 52, respectively.

Then, in mid-August 1944, came the major reorganisation within the Luftwaffe's fighter arm that was to see every *Jagdgruppe's* establishment increased from three *Staffeln* to four. Thus, after several weeks operating on attachment under their original designations, the above *Staffeln* were officially incorporated into the *Geschwader* as 8. and 12./JG 3. This resulted in an immediate influx of 'ready-made' aces and *Experten* into the ranks of JG 3 – none more illustrious, perhaps, than centurion Leutnant Hans Waldmann, holder of the Knight's Cross, who now found himself the *Staffelkapitän* of 8./JG 3. Yet even he could make little impact on the overpowering might of the western Allies. In II./JG 3's final days in France he managed to account for just three P-47s. This had taken his score to 132, where it would remain until his departure to join JG 7 three months later.

It was while the *Geschwader* was engaged over Normandy that it received its next batch of decorations. Two of the six awards announced during June and July were posthumous – a Knight's Cross for Major Klaus Quaet-Faslem on 9 June and Oak Leaves for Oberleutnant Otto Wessling on 20 July. Four more Knight's Crosses were conferred upon pilots with scores ranging from 34 to 70 (see Appendix 1 for details).

And meanwhile, what of the *Stab* and the other two *Gruppen*? When the Allies invaded Normandy JG 3 was in the care of an acting *Kommodore*. A replacement for the late Karl-Heinz 'Tutti' Müller had been named on

Pilots of III./JG 3 drawn up in a fairly leisurely manner in front of the *Gruppe's* chateau HQ at Marcilly-la-Campagne, south of Evreux, on 10 June 1944. Among them, front rank first left, is the unit's current highest scorer, Oberleutnant Raimund Koch (the *Kapitän* of 8. *Staffel*) who had claimed his 21st victory – a P-51 – just three days earlier. With a final total standing at 26, Koch would be killed in a mid-air collision with his wingman on 2 November 1944. Two along from Koch, with his face bandaged, is the now Oberfähnrich (Officer Aspirant) Wolfgang Rentsch

1 June. This was to be the Swords-wearing double-centurion Major Heinz Bär, one of the true – if somewhat unpredictable – 'greats' of the Luftwaffe fighter arm. But 'Pritzl' Bär did not arrive to take up office until 10 June, whereupon he promptly set about converting the *Stab* from its Bf 109Gs to his preferred Fw 190s. As a consequence, *Stab* JG 3 saw little combat over Normandy. It lost a young oberfähnrich in a dogfight near Caen on 24 July and its only success of the campaign was the P-51 downed by the *Kommodore* southeast of Chartres on 7 August. This was Heinz Bär's 203rd victory of the war to date.

Hauptmann Helmut Mertens' I./JG 3 did not have time to see much action over the invasion front either. It had arrived in France on 11 June and was back in Germany for rest and re-equipment just 16 days later. In the interim it had been credited with nine Allied fighters destroyed, including two P-47s claimed by Hauptmann Ernst Laube of the *Gruppenstab* (which had raised his total to 18). Against this the unit lost seven pilots killed, among them one of the last of the *Geschwader's* real 'old hares'. Semi--centurion Oberfeldwebel Gustav Dilling of 3. *Staffel*, whose first victory had been an RAF Blenheim IV back in September 1940, was shot down while attacking a formation of B-26 Marauders in the Caen area on 14 June.

If I./JG 3's deployment to the Normandy front had been brief, then IV. *Gruppe's* was positively fleeting. Touching down at Dreux, west of Paris, on 8 June, it departed again after just five days! This quick turnaround was presumably due to someone in the corridors of power suddenly waking up to the fact that the invasion beachheads – where most of the air action involved medium- to low-level fighter combat – were no place for a specialised *Gruppe* of heavily armoured Focke-Wulfs, whose pilots had been specifically trained to bring down high-altitude heavy bombers.

IV.(*Sturm*)/JG 3's foray into France therefore resulted in the loss of just one aircraft (which had crashed during transfer) and a single victory. The P-51 claimed on the evening of 10 June was the first for future ace Unteroffizier Harry Wald of 16. *Staffel*.

By the second week of July 1944, Major Karl-Heinz Langer's III./JG 3 had retired some 55 kilometres to take up temporary residence on 'Airfield C', a landing ground outside Sours to the southeast of Chartres. Here, it was visited by *Generalfeldmarschall* Hugo Sperrle, GOC *Luftflotte* 3 (right). Also pictured, in shirtsleeve order, is Major Heinz Bär, JG 3's new *Geschwaderkommodore*

CHAPTER NINE

RETREAT AND DEFEAT

The post-Normandy fortunes of the *Geschwader's* four *Gruppen* were to vary greatly. II. and III./JG 3 had remained in action over the invasion front for very nearly three months, not leaving France until German forces had retreated back across the Seine late in August 1944.

The campaign had cost the two *Gruppen* dearly. Between them they had lost almost 100 pilots killed, missing or captured, plus an even greater number of aircraft destroyed or damaged on the ground. It was an experience from which they would never fully recover. Admittedly, their losses in men and machines were soon made good, but the young pilots now being turned out by the training schools were ill-prepared for the crucible of combat. They would stand little chance of survival against an experienced enemy. And by the time II. and III./JG 3 returned to operations in the autumn, that enemy was not only experienced, he had gained complete mastery of the skies over Germany.

I./JG 3 had returned from its 16-day sojourn on the Normandy front in far better shape. Yet even its pilots would need four or five weeks of rest and recuperation before resuming their homeland defence duties.

All of which left just the heavily armoured Fw 190s of Hauptmann Wilhelm Moritz's IV.(*Sturm*)/JG 3 – whose involvement in France had

Major Wilhelm Moritz, right, who was to command IV.(*Sturm*)/JG 3 from April to December 1944 – adding 11 heavy bombers to his overall score and winning the Knight's Cross in the process – takes time off one evening to play a few hands of *Skat*

The amazing 49(!) victories credited to IV.(*Sturm*)/JG 3 on 18 July 1944 included nine 'firsts' and produced three new five-victory aces. The day's action also enabled Leutnant Oskar Romm, the recently appointed *Kapitän* of 12. *Staffel*, to claim his first three kills with JG 3, thereby raising his overall total to 80

Wounded during the mission of 18 July (which netted him his 36th, and final, victory), Leutnant Hans Weik, the *Kapitän* of 10. *Staffel*, visited his old unit – redesignated in the meantime to become 16.(*Sturm*)/JG 3 – at Schongau the following month. The line-up includes (from second left, with total JG 3 victories in brackets) Unteroffiziere Erhard Kröber (4) and Kurt Bolz (4), Leutnant Weik (36), Leutnant Walther Hagenah (16), Feldwebel Hans Schäfer (18), Unteroffiziere Willi Vohl (3), Hubert Drdla (18) and Günther Heinig (5). Standing in shirt sleeves at far right is Hauptfeldwebel Maxeiner, the *Staffel Spiess*, or senior warrant officer

lasted a mere matter of hours – as the only 'Udet' *Gruppe* to fly Defence of the Reich operations during the late summer of 1944.

And an extremely good job its pilots made of it too. On some days the number of enemy aircraft they brought down equalled, and occasionally even exceeded, the totals claimed by the *Geschwader's* three original *Gruppen* during the opening heydays of *Barbarossa* three years earlier. Their achievements are made even more noteworthy by the fact that their

Portrayed here as an oberfeldwebel, Ekkehard Tichy had claimed the first of his 25 victories as a leutnant with 9./JG 3 on the eastern front in May 1943. Appointed *Kapitän* of his *Staffel* six months later, he was wounded in action against B-17s on 18 March 1944. Returning to duty as an oberleutnant and the *Staffelkapitän* of 10.(*Sturm*)/JG 3 on 3 August 1944, he achieved his final four kills – all Fortresses – in less than a fortnight, despatching the last on 16 August by ramming

opponents were not penny-packets of poorly armed and often decidedly inferior Red Air Force machines, but armadas of high-flying heavy bombers bristling with defensive armament and protected by near impenetrable screens of escorting fighters.

This is what they had been trained for, of course – to bring down the Americans' four-engined bombers – but the figures are nonetheless impressive. In the six months from mid-June to mid-December 1944 the *Gruppe* was credited with 250 US aircraft destroyed. And with the exception of 13 fighters, every single one of their victims was a heavy bomber. More than 50 of those bombers provided 'firsts' for young pilots just starting out on their combat careers. It was an inescapable sign of the times, however, that only 14 of those new pilots survived to score another four or more kills to evolve into fledgling aces.

In addition to the many youngsters fresh out of training school who made up the bulk of its numbers, IV.(*Sturm*)/JG 3 also included among its ranks a dozen or so more experienced pilots transferred in from other units (including those of *Sturmstaffel* 1, which had by now been incorporated into the *Gruppe* as its new 11. *Staffel*). These men nearly all boasted totals approaching, or already into, double figures. The top scorer of all, however – and by a long margin – was the *Kommandeur* himself.

On 7 July 1944, in the unit's first major action since returning from Normandy, Hauptmann Wilhelm Moritz had claimed one of the 22 Liberators credited to the *Gruppe* in what the German propaganda machine was quick to dub the 'Battle of Oschersleben'. This had taken

Hauptmann Moritz's score to 40. No 41 went down 11 days later when the Fifteenth Air Force flew up from Italy to attack targets in southern Germany, including IV. *Gruppe's* own airfield at Memmingen.

Despite the damage and fatalities suffered on the ground, 18 July 1944 was to prove the most successful day in the *Gruppe's* entire history. By its close an incredible 47(!) B-17s and two P-51s had been accounted for. It also provided the unit with a new top scorer. Knight's Cross-wearing Leutnant Oskar Romm, a long-serving member of JG 51, had been appointed *Staffelkapitän* of 12.(*Sturm*)/JG 3 after the previous incumbent, ten-victory Oberleutnant Hans Rachner, was killed in the 'Battle of Oschersleben'. On 18 July 'Ossi' Romm was responsible for downing a brace of B-17s and one of the two Mustangs destroyed. The latter raised his overall total to exactly 80.

Romm's previous *Staffel*, 2./JG 51, had been one of those withdrawn from the eastern front to bolster the Defence of the Reich order of battle. For some weeks past it had been attached to IV.(*Sturm*)/JG 3, and in mid-August, as part of the major restructuring of the Luftwaffe's fighter forces, it was officially incorporated into the *Gruppe* as its new 16. *Staffel*. It brought with it several more ready-made aces, the highest scoring of whom was its *Kapitän*, the recent semi-centurion Oberleutnant Horst Haase.

A founder member of the original *Sturmstaffel* 1, Feldwebel Gerhard Vivroux scored five victories – all B-17s – with that unit prior to its incorporation into JG 3 (initially as 11. *Staffel*, and then as 14. *Staffel*). With these latter he took his final total to 11 before being seriously wounded in a dogfight with P-51s south of Stettin on 6 October. He died in hospital 19 days later

Although this fresh blood enabled the *Gruppe* to continue inflicting substantial losses on the US bomber streams, it was never again to repeat its successes of July 1944. On only three occasions between August and mid-December did its pilots manage to bring down more than 20 of the enemy's 'heavies' in any one day. Those four months were marked instead by lengthening casualty lists, and the losses were not just confined to the inexperienced tyros either. About a dozen aces also fell victim to the bombers' defensive fire, or their escorting fighters, during this period. Among them were several of the 'newcomers' to the *Gruppe*. Feldwebel Gerhard Vivroux, for example, a member of the original *Sturmstaffel* 1 – now 14.(*Sturm*)/JG 3 – had crashed on landing back at Alteno after being wounded in a dogfight with P-51s close to the Baltic coast on 6 October. Vivroux, who had added six more enemy aircraft to the five already claimed while serving with the *Sturmstaffel*, succumbed to his injuries on 25 October.

Hauptmann Moritz also lost three of his four *Staffelkapitäne* into the bargain. The first to be killed was 25-victory Oberleutnant Ekkehard Tichy of 13.(*Sturm*)/JG 3, his fighter going down after it had collided with a B-17 to the northeast of Schweinfurt on 16 August. 14.(*Sturm*)/JG 3's Oberleutnant Werner Gerth also claimed his 27th and final victim – another B-17 – by ramming (whether intentional or not, is no longer clear) during the mission of 2 November that cost the *Gruppe* ten pilots killed or missing. And it was exactly one month later, on 2 December, that Oberleutnant Wilhelm-Erich Volkmann, the *Staffelkapitän* of 16.(*Sturm*)/JG 3, claimed his fifth. This was one of the 22 Liberators credited to the *Gruppe* during a running battle west of the Rhine on that date. It was also to be Volkmann's last victory. Post-war records reveal two facts – the actual number of B-24s that failed to return from the raid on Bingen marshalling yards was 11, and Oberleutnant Volkmann was one of five pilots lost to the *Gruppe* in the action.

By this time the other three *Gruppen* had also resumed operations. The first was I./JG 3, which had begun flying missions out of Gütersloh late in July. But its pilots had little opportunity to match IV. *Gruppe's* anti-bomber successes for, in line with most of the other Bf 109-equipped units engaged in Defence of the Reich duties at this stage of the war, I./JG 3's primary role was to protect the Fw 190s of the *Sturmgruppen* from enemy fighters. And given the sheer numbers of those enemy fighters not only escorting the bomber streams, but now roaming almost at will into the furthest recesses of the Reich, it was to prove no easy task.

In the last five months of 1944 the *Gruppe* succeeded in bringing down just 44 Allied aircraft (only six of which were USAAF heavy bombers). And almost a third of that total was claimed on one day alone (12 December) when, in addition to a single P-51, I./JG 3's pilots were credited with a surprising haul – 13 RAF Lancaster bombers! Among the claimants (nearly half of whom were 'first-timers') were two *Staffelkapitäne*. Taking his overall score to 38, 2./JG 3's Oberleutnant Walter Brandt got one, while 4. *Staffel's* Leutnant Franz Ruhl accounted for a pair, bringing him up to 37. Once again, however, post-war records show that these claims must be treated with caution, as only eight Lancasters were, in fact, lost in the 12 December daylight raid on the Witten steelyards in the Ruhr valley.

The pilots in this photograph of 14.(*Sturm*)/JG 3 taken in late 1944 accounted for six of the 30 B-26 Marauders credited to IV. *Gruppe* on 23 December. Identifiable among them are several current or future aces, including Unteroffiziere Helmut Keune and Oskar Bösch (first and second right), *Staffelkapitän* Leutnant Gotthard Glaubig (tall figure, sixth from right) and Unteroffizier Raab (in life-jacket, standing seventh right beside Glaubig)

Inevitably, I. Gruppe's 44 victories came at a cost. Between August and December I./JG 3 suffered more than 100 pilot casualties, 85 of them killed, missing or captured. Among those killed were two *Gruppenkommandeure* and three *Staffelkapitäne* (most of whom, however, had been transferred in from other units and had scored few, if any kills while serving with JG 3). Even Hauptmann Horst Haase, hitherto the *Staffelkapitän* of 16.(*Sturm*)/JG 3, who had 56 victories to his credit when he assumed command of the *Gruppe* on 30 October, had been unable to add to that total before losing his life in a mid-air collision with his wingman in heavy cloud near the Dutch border on 26 November. His successor at the head of the *Gruppe* lasted a mere five days, being one of the eight pilots lost to US fighters on 2 December.

It was during the course of one week late in October, incidentally, that the *Geschwader* had received its last batch of Knight's Crosses – four being awarded to pilots with scores ranging from 19 to 56 (for details see Appendix 1). None of these decorations had gone to II. *Gruppe*. In fact, little at all is known of II./JG 3's successes during its seven weeks of Defence of the Reich operations, which were to last from early October until the end of November. One source suggests that it may have claimed up to ten victories during this period. What *is* known is that by the end of it the unit had suffered 19 pilots killed – 12 on 2 November alone! One of the dozen lost in the huge, sprawling dogfight near Leipzig on that date was Leutnant Walter Becker, the *Kapitän* of 6. *Staffel*.

Hauptmann Karl-Heinz Langer's III./JG 3 did not return to Defence of the Reich operations until late November. In its first three weeks the unit managed to bring down just two enemy machines (both 'firsts' for the two 9. *Staffel* pilots involved), but lost nine of its own number killed, including two *Staffelkapitäne*, in so doing.

Then, on 16 December 1944, a virtually 'impenetrable blanket of bad weather' descended over England, bringing the Eighth Air Force's activities to an almost total, if temporary, halt. It was the window of opportunity that Hitler had been waiting for. He unleashed 21 divisions (seven of them armoured) in a surprise counter-offensive out of the Belgian Ardennes – the very area from which he had launched his *Blitzkrieg* in the west over four years earlier.

The 'Battle of the Bulge', as it has since become known, brought about an immediate change of role for the pilots of I. and III./JG 3, although, in reality, they were to experience very little change at all. Tasked with supporting and protecting the ground troops as they fought their way west towards the River Meuse (more shades of the *Blitzkrieg*!), the two *Gruppen* had merely exchanged the high-altitude escort fighters of the Eighth Air Force – still pinned to their British bases by the atrocious local weather conditions – for the low-level fighters of the USAAF's Ninth Air Force and the RAF's 2nd Tactical Air Force (TAF), which by this time were already operating from airfields on the Continent.

During the latter half of December I./JG 3 was credited with just six Allied fighters, and the cost to the *Gruppe* had been exorbitant – 17 of its pilots killed, missing or captured, plus others wounded or injured. Among the casualties were the two *Staffelkapitäne* who were currently the *Gruppe's* leading scorers (although neither one of them had added to his total since their brush with the RAF Lancasters two weeks earlier). Leutnant Franz Ruhl, the 37-victory *Kapitän* of 4. *Staffel*, fell victim to US fighters during a *freie Jagd* sweep along the northern shoulder of the 'Bulge' on 24 December. Still one ahead of Ruhl, 2./JG 3's Leutnant Walter Brandt was injured 24 hours later when his machine somersaulted while taking off from Paderborn.

III./JG 3's involvement in the 'Bulge' fighting was only marginally less costly – 15 of its pilots were killed or reported missing. But against this the unit accounted for 13 enemy aircraft, including a trio of B-26 Marauders brought down northeast of St Vith on 23 December. Moreover, the *Gruppe's* two most successful pilots added to their scores during the battle, and emerged from it unscathed. Leutnant Oskar Zimmermann, the *Staffelkapitän* of 9./JG 3, downed a P-47 on 18 December, which took his overall total to 29. And Hauptmann Karl-Heinz Langer was responsible for one of the three Marauders on the 23rd, before then also claiming a P-47 four days later. These were the *Gruppenkommandeur's* 24th and 25th kills.

True to recent form, however, it was the Fw 190s of IV. *Gruppe* that achieved by far the best results during the short-lived Ardennes campaign, claiming 63 enemy aircraft destroyed – well over two-thirds of them on two consecutive days alone!

It was on 23 December, after downing a trio of P-47s in the Bonn area, that the *Gruppe* chanced upon a large formation of unescorted B-26s retiring from bombing a railway viaduct north of Remagen. Employing their proven *Sturm* tactics of attacking the enemy from the rear, the Fw 190 pilots closed in on the Marauders before letting fly with their heavy cannon. In a running fight lasting less than 15 minutes, the pilots of IV.(*Sturm*)/JG 3 claimed no fewer than 30 of the twin-engined bombers. Two of them provided fifth victories for Unteroffiziere Hubert Drdla and Helmut Keune of 13. and 14. *Staffeln*, respectively. Others increased the scores of existing aces. Feldwebel Harry Wald of 16.(*Sturm*)/JG 3 was

Hauptmann Wolfgang Kosse had undergone what can only be described as a roller-coaster career before being appointed *Staffelkapitän* of 13. (*Sturm*)/JG 3 in October 1944. His five victories with IV. *Gruppe* – all of them Allied fighters, the last downed during the Battle of the Bulge – made him one of JG 3's last known aces

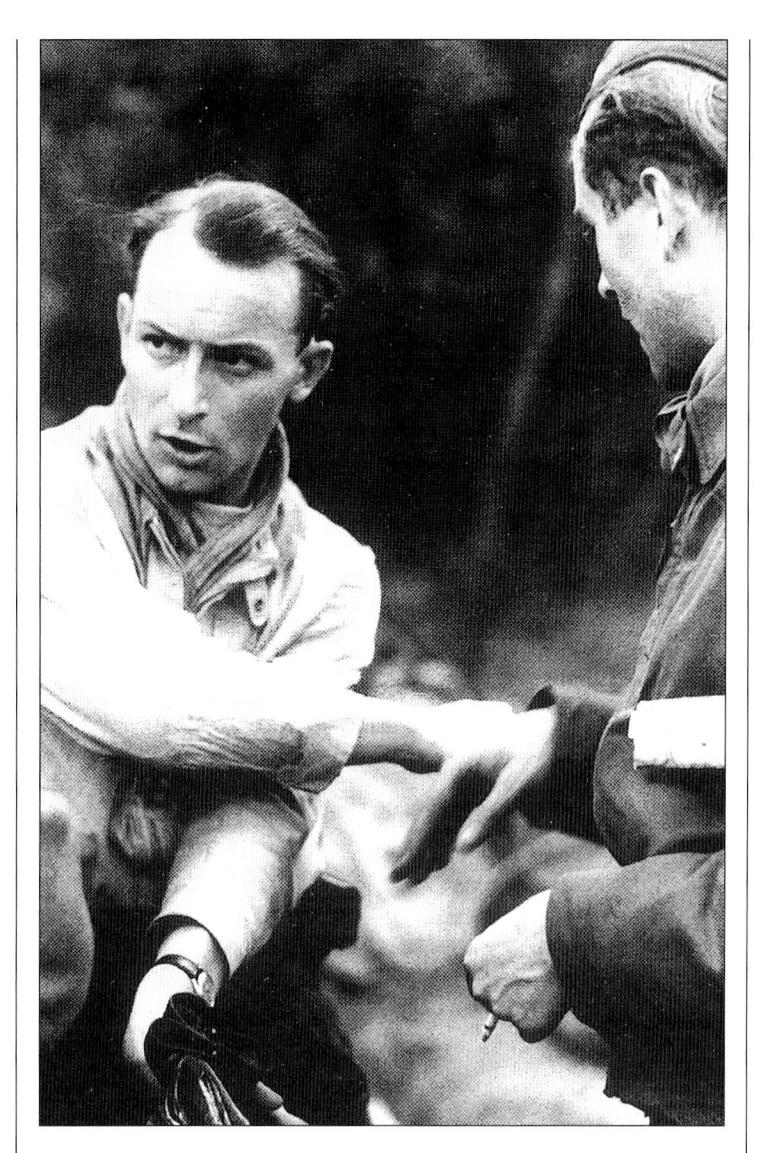

credited with three and his *Staffelkapitän*, Leutnant Siegfried Müller, with two, taking them to 13 apiece.

The following day saw the arrival of a high-pressure area across northwest Europe. The skies finally cleared and the murky conditions over the Eighth Air Force's English airfields lifted, allowing the Allies' UK-based heavy bombers to intervene for the first time in the Battle of the Bulge. The result was the largest single heavy bomber strike of the war, with more than 1800 American and 800 British aircraft targeting airfields and communications centres across a wide area of western Germany to the immediate rear of the ground fighting.

As part of the Luftwaffe's response to this devastating onslaught, IV.(*Sturm*)/JG 3's claims for ten B-17s (plus a subsequent quartet of RAF Typhoons) was creditable, but of little real significance. Nor did the *Gruppe's* 63 successes of the Ardennes campaign as a whole come cheaply – 26 of its pilots would be killed, reported missing or captured, among them the *Gruppenkommandeur* and two *Staffelkapitäne*.

One of the latter, 13.(*Sturm*)/JG 3's Hauptmann Wolfgang Kosse, had been the *Gruppe's* highest overall scorer at the time of his loss. He had claimed four kills during the Battle of the Bulge, the last pair being two of the Typhoons shot down as the Fw 190s were returning from their assault on the B-17s on 24 December. The two RAF fighter-bombers had taken Kosse's final total to 28. He himself then fell victim to other Typhoons during the engagement near Liège, thus marking the end of a long and eventful career.

Wolfgang Kosse had claimed his first 11 victories as a leutnant with JG 26 over France and on the Channel front during 1941-42, before being transferred to JG 5 in the far north. Here, he had added another seven to his score while rising to the rank of hauptmann and position of *Staffelkapitän*, only to be summarily reduced to the ranks for 'abuse of his authority'. As a flieger (airman – the lowest of the low in the Luftwaffe) Kosse had then volunteered for service with *Sturmstaffel* 1, gaining a further five victories and promotion to gefreiter before being reinstated to the rank of hauptmann and appointed *Staffelkapitän* of 13.(*Sturm*)/JG 3.

By the end of 1944 it was clear that the Battle of the Bulge, Hitler's last great gamble in the west, had failed. But the Luftwaffe still had one final blow of its own to deliver. Operation *Bodenplatte* ('Baseplate') was an ambitious plan designed to destroy the bulk of the enemy's continental-based tactical air power by staging a massed, coordinated attack on its airfields in France and the Low Countries. Involving almost the whole

Although he claimed just three victories during his seven-month tenure of command as *Geschwaderkommodore*, Heinz 'Pritzl' Bär (left) more than merits inclusion here as the only double-centurion ever to serve with JG 3

of the Defence of the Reich organisation – some 12 *Geschwader* in all, plus a number of smaller units – *Bodenplatte* was launched at first light on 1 January 1945.

Each *Geschwader* had been assigned its own specific target airfield and, in terms of enemy machines destroyed on the ground, JG 3's attack on Eindhoven, in the Netherlands, was among the most successful of the entire operation. Nearly 50 aircraft, the majority of them Typhoons, were totally destroyed and some 60 others damaged.

The day's results in the air were far less impressive. Against the loss of 17 of its own pilots (including three *Staffelkapitäne*) killed, missing or captured, the *Geschwader* was credited with just nine enemy fighters shot down. Two of them fell to Oberstleutnant Heinz Bär. Initially identified as Tempests (but almost certainly a pair of RCAF Typhoons), these were the first kills to be claimed by the *Geschwaderkommodore* since the P-51 brought down back in August, and completed the trio of victories he achieved while at the head of JG 3. With his overall score still standing at 205, 'Pritzl' Bär would relinquish command of the *Geschwader* in mid-February 1945 to take over an Me 262 jet unit.

I. *Gruppe's* sole aerial contribution to *Bodenplatte* was the single Spitfire claimed by Oberfeldwebel Friedrich Hameister, the acting-*Staffelkapitän* of 4./JG 3, who was himself hit by anti-aircraft fire only moments later. He survived the subsequent crash landing to join four of his fellow NCOs in captivity. Hameister's Spitfire had been a 'first'. In contrast, the 'Tempest' (another Typhoon?) credited to Leutnant Oskar Zimmermann, the *Staffelkapitän* of 9./JG 3, had taken his total to 30. III. *Gruppe's* only other success was a Canadian Spitfire, which was number seven for 10. *Staffel's* Oberfeldwebel Robert Reisner. On the debit side, III./JG 3's three losses – all brought down by flak – included ten-victory Leutnant Hans-Ulrich Jung also of 10. *Staffel*.

IV.(*Sturm*)/JG 3's five losses were offset to some extent by their four victories. Among them, a Spitfire provided number ten for Feldwebel Oskar Bösch of 14.(*Sturm*)/JG 3, while a Typhoon apiece took 16. *Staffel's* Leutnant Siegfried Müller and Feldwebel Harry Wald to 14 each.

Although *Bodenplatte* had, without doubt, inflicted considerable damage on the units of the Ninth Air Force and 2nd TAF, that damage was mainly material, which could quickly be made good. Such was not the case for the Luftwaffe, however. It had suffered the loss of more than 250 pilots, many of whom – especially the 19 experienced formation leaders among them – would be very hard to replace. A Pyrrhic victory of epic proportions, *Bodenplatte* had achieved little more than to hasten the end of Luftwaffe fighter operations in the west.

With the collapse of his counter-offensive in the Ardennes, Hitler virtually abandoned the western front to its fate. By mid-January 1945 his attention had become firmly focussed on the east, where the Red Army was already threatening to overrun the Reich's border provinces. And, after one final major confrontation with the Americans on 14 January (during which US fighter pilots claimed another 174 Luftwaffe machines shot down, among them six-victory Unteroffizier Helmut Keune of IV./JG 3), it was to the east that Hitler now directed what was left of his fighter forces, including JG 3, in the desperate hope of stemming the Red Army tide.

Although information about the *Geschwader's* final three months on the eastern front is rather sketchy, some details *are* known. After Oberstleutnant Heinz Bär's transfer to the jet arm, command of JG 3 passed into the capable hands of Major Werner Schroer, an Oak Leaves-wearing centurion with long years of service with JG 27 behind him. During March and April 1945 it was Major Schroer who was to claim all 12 of the *Geschwaderstab's* last recorded victories. These raised his overall total to 114, and won him the Swords in the process.

The 14 victories attributed to I./JG 3 in February and March 1945 included a threesome for Leutnant Walter Brandt, the *Kapitän* of 2. *Staffel*, during a lengthy battle with a large formation of fighter-escorted Pe-2s southeast of Stettin on 3 March. Brandt was himself wounded in the engagement and forced to belly-land. The pair of Pe-2s and single Lavochkin fighter (Nos 40-42) are thought to have been his final kills, for although he soon recovered from his injuries and was then transferred to II./JG 3, being appointed the *Kapitän* of 7. *Staffel* in early April, he is not known to have achieved any further successes during the last four weeks of the war. In fact, very little at all is known about the activities of II. *Gruppe* between March and May 1945, other than the fact that it suffered the loss of at least nine of its pilots killed or missing in action against the Soviets.

The original II./JG 3 had been redesignated as I./JG 7 back at the end of November 1944, and it should perhaps be pointed out that the II. *Gruppe* transferred to the Baltic coast three months later was an entirely different unit formed from a disbanded Ju 88 *Kampfgruppe*.

III./JG 3's operations over the same area from late January to late April 1945 are thought to have netted its pilots close on 90 victories. Details are

With 16.(*Sturm*)/JG 3 having been disbanded on 10 March 1945, this photograph of Oberleutnant Oskar Romm, the *Kommandeur* of IV. *Gruppe*, and his three remaining *Staffelkapitäne* at Prenzlau, 80 kilometres north of Berlin, must have been taken some time between that date and 25 April 1945 – the day on which 'Ossi' Romm was wounded and the *Gruppe* moved to Tutow. From left are Leutnant Siegfried Müller (13. *Staffel*), Hauptmann Erich Kron (*Gruppenstab* HQ), Oberleutnant Romm, Leutnant Karl-Dieter Hecker (15. *Staffel*) and Leutnant Willi Unger (14. *Staffel*)

again sparse, but this total did include Nos 26-30 for *Gruppenkommandeur* Hauptmann Karl-Heinz Langer, which earned him the Knight's Cross on 20 April. It also produced at least three new five-victory aces. In fact, the Yak-9 downed by Leutnant Paul Angst, the *Staffelkapitän* of 10./JG 3, on 24 April could well make him JG 3's very last ace of all.

These successes cost the *Gruppe* 28 pilots killed or missing, plus a further eight wounded or injured. Among those killed were two *Staffelkapitäne*, plus six others who deliberately sacrificed their lives in suicide dives on the Oder bridges on 16 April – the day the Red Army launched its last great assault on Berlin.

Once again, as in the recent past, it was the Fw 190s of IV. *Gruppe* that were to dominate this final chapter in the *Geschwader's* history. Although far from complete, records indicate that IV.(*Sturm*)/JG 3 (the unit appears to have retained its *Sturm* appellation to the bitter end, even though its specialised anti-bomber operations had long ceased, and it was now being employed solely in the ground-attack role) claimed well over 100 victories from mid-February to the close of the war. The price paid was 29 pilots killed, missing or captured, plus a further eight wounded. By far the highest scorer at this time was Oberleutnant Oskar Romm. When appointed *Gruppenkommandeur* on 17 February his total was already standing at 86. He was to add another six – the last an Il-2 *Shturmovik* downed on 21 March – before being injured when forced to belly-land his Fw 190D 'Long-nose' on 24 April.

'Ossi' Romm's successor at the head of IV. *Gruppe*, Knight's Cross-holder Hauptmann Gerhard Koall, previously of JG 54, lasted just three days in office. He was brought down by flak while strafing Soviet troops northeast of Neubrandenburg on 27 April. Hauptmann Koall was in turn replaced by an even more illustrious figure, 174-victory, Oak Leaves-wearing Hauptmann Günther Schack. A long-time member of JG 51, he was brought in to command IV.(*Sturm*)/JG 3 for the last eight days of the war. But it was a small group of NCO pilots – some of them 'old hares', others relative novices – who were to exact by far the greatest toll on the enemy during this final round of the four-year fight against the Red Air Force.

Incredibly, not only did a new trio of five-victory aces emerge at this late stage, but two pilots, both of 13. *Staffel*, went even further by achieving 'five-in-one-day'! Unteroffizier Ferdinand Löschenkohl was credited with five Pe-2s near Stettin on 15 March, and then claimed three more of the same type on 1 April to take his final tally to 11. Feldwebel Hubert Drdla's five – a quartet of Pe-2s plus a Yak-3 (Nos 14-18 for Drdla) – were also claimed on 1 April.

The most successful NCO pilot during this period was Oberfeldwebel Walter Kutz. Starting with three Pe-2s downed on 15 March (in the same engagement that had given Unteroffizier Löschenkohl his five), Kutz's total had risen to 17 by the time Germany surrendered less than eight weeks later. Others who ended the war with double figures were Feldwebeln Oskar Bösch with 18 and Harry Wald with 25. Incidentally, it was Wald's first kill, a P-51, that had provided IV.(*Sturm*)/JG 3 with its only invasion front victory nearly a year earlier.

The current highest-scoring NCO of all, *Sturmstaffel* 1 veteran Feldwebel Willi Maximowitz, now of 14.(*Sturm*)/JG 3, did not survive to see the end of hostilities. Maximowitz, with 27-victories to his name, and his entire *Schwarm* (section of four aircraft) all fell victim to Red Air Force fighters near Berlin on 20 April 1945. This same date also saw the only non-Soviet victory to be credited to the *Gruppe* since its transfer to the eastern front some three months before when 15. *Staffel's* Feldwebel Reinhold Hoffmann claimed his 11th, and last, kill – a Belgian-flown Spitfire of the RAF engaged in an early evening sweep of the Berlin area.

Prior to this, during the first week of April, two of the *Gruppe's Staffelkapitäne*, 13.(*Sturm*)/JG 3's Leutnant Siegfried Müller and 14.(*Sturm*)/JG 3's Leutnant Willi Unger (whose current scores were standing at 17 and 23 respectively), had been posted to the Me 262-equipped JG 7. Willi Unger's replacement at the head of 14. *Staffel* was Leutnant Herbert Bareuther, yet another ex-member of JG 51, and it is with this 'newcomer' that the story of the aces of *Jagdgeschwader* 3 'Udet' comes to a close.

The then Unteroffizier Herbert Bareuther had claimed his first victory with JG 51 on 22 June 1941 – the opening day of *Barbarossa*. By the time he assumed command of 14.(*Sturm*)/JG 3 on 2 April 1945 that figure had risen to 44. In the next four weeks he would be credited with a further 11 enemy aircraft destroyed before he was himself killed while carrying out a low-level attack on Soviet troops advancing west of the Oder. As an oberfeldwebel back in February 1944, Herbert Bareuther had won the German Cross in Gold. Some references suggest that he received the Knight's Cross during the closing days of the war. But whether this was conferred prior to his loss on 30 April 1945 or awarded posthumously is not certain. As with so much information relating to JG 3's activities in those final chaotic weeks leading up to the German surrender, details are no longer available.

Another veteran of *Sturmstaffel* 1, 27-victory Feldwebel Willi Maximowitz of 14.(*Sturm*)/JG 3 failed to return from a mission over the Oder front to the east of Berlin on 20 April 1945

APPENDICES

APPENDIX 1: Decorations (Knight's Cross and Above) Awarded to Serving Members of *Jagdgeschwader* 3 'Udet'

Date	Name/Rank	Award	Number of Kills
18/9/40	Lützow, Hptm Günther	KC	15
6/2/41	Oesau, Hptm Walter	OL	40
9/7/41	von Hahn, Hptm Hans	KC	21
9/7/41	Keller, Hptm Lothar	KC(†)	20
15/7/41	Oesau, Hptm Walter	S	80
20/7/41	Lützow, Maj Günther	OL	42
27/7/41	Olejnik, Oblt Robert	KC	32
30/7/41	Bauer, Oblt Viktor	KC	34
12/8/41	Meckel, Oblt Helmut	KC	25
12/8/41	Bucholz, Oblt Max	KC	27
12/8/41	Sochatzy, Oblt Kurt	KC	38
30/8/41	Beyer, Oblt Franz	KC	32
4/9/41	Schentke, Obfw Georg	KC	30
4/9/41	Stechmann, Obfw Hans	KC	30
18/9/41	Schmidt, Oblt Winfried	KC	19
18/9/41	Gollob, Hptm Gordon M	KC	42
5/10/41	Rohwer, Ltn Detlev	KC	28
11/10/41	Lützow, Maj Günther	S	92
26/10/41	Gollob, Hptm Gordon M	OL	85
4/11/41	Michalek, Oblt Georg	KC	36
4/11/41	Ohlrogge, Fw Walter	KC	39
3/5/42	von Boremski, Obfw Eberhard	KC	43
3/5/42	Hübner, Ltn Ekhard	KC(†)	47
9/5/42	Schleef, Fw Hans	KC	41
1/7/42	Brändle, Hptm Kurt	KC	49
26/7/42	Bauer, Oblt Viktor	OL	102
23/8/42	Fuss, Ltn Hans	KC	60
27/8/42	Brändle, Hptm Kurt	OL	100
3/9/42	Wessling, Obfw Otto	KC	50
4/9/42	Mertens, Oblt Helmut	KC	50
9/9/42	Wilcke, Hptm Wolf-Dietrich	OL	100
12/9/42	Lemke, Ltn Wilhelm	KC	50
19/9/42	Heckmann, Obfw Alfred	KC	50
19/9/42	Lucas, Fw Werner	KC	50
2/10/42	Engfer, Fw Siegfried	KC	52
2/10/42	Kemethmüller, Fw Heinz	KC	59
29/10/42	Schwaiger, Uffz Franz	KC	52
9/12/42	Ewald, Maj Wolfgang	KC	50
21/12/42	Häfner, Ltn Ludwig	KC(†)	52
21/12/42	Münster, Fw Leopold	KC	52
23/12/42	Kirschner, Ltn Joachim	KC	51
23/12/42	Rüffler, Fw Helmut	KC	50
28/12/42	Wilcke, Maj Wolf-Dietrich	S	155
7/4/43	Ebener, Fw Kurt	KC	52
1/6/43	Ettel, Ltn Wolf	KC	120
2/8/43	Kirschner, Oblt Joachim	OL	170

Date	Name	Award	Kills
29/8/43	Bitsch, Oblt Emil	KC	105
25/11/43	Lemke, Hptm Wilhelm	OL	130
5/2/44	Frielinghaus, Oblt Gustav	KC	74
11/3/44	Dahl, Maj Walther	KC	64
12/5/44	Münster, Ltn Leopold	OL(†)	95
9/6/44	Quaet-Faslem, Maj Klaus	KC(†)	49
8/7/44	Grünberg, Ltn Hans	KC	70
18/7/44	Moritz, Hptm Wilhelm	KC	41
20/7/44	Wessling, Oblt Otto	OL(†)	83
27/7/44	Ruhl, Ltn Franz	KC	34
27/7/44	Weik, Ltn Hans	KC	36
23/10/44	Unger, Fhj-Fw Willi	KC	19
24/10/44	Haase, Hptm Horst	KC	56
29/10/44	Gerth, Oblt Werner	KC	26
29/10/44	Zimmermann, Ltn Oskar	KC	28
9/12/44	Neumann, Fw Klaus	KC	31
27/1/45	Tichy, Hptm Ekkehard	KC(†)	25
16/4/45	Schroer, Maj Werner	S	108
20/4/45	Langer, Maj Karl-Heinz	KC	29
??/4/45	Bareuther, Ltn Herbert	KC	(?)

Notes and abbreviations

Number of Kills refers to the pilot's score at the time the award was first announced, although the recipient may have added to his total by the time of the presentation

KC – Knight's Cross
OL – Oak Leaves
S – Swords
(†) – (Posthumous)

APPENDIX 2: Aces of *Jagdgeschwader* 3 'Udet'*

Victories with JG 3	Name/Rank	*Gruppe(n)*	Date of Fifth Victory	Total Score	Other JG(s)	Fate
175	Kirschner, Ltn Joachim	I/II	29/5/42	188	27	KIA 17/12/43
137	Brändle, Hptm Kurt	II	26/5/42	172	53	KIA 3/11/43
131	Lemke, Ltn Wilhelm	II/III	29/6/41	131	–	KIA 4/12/43
124	Wilcke, Hptm Wolf-Dietrich	GS	30/6/42	162	53	KIA 23/3/44
120	Ettel, Ltn Wolf	II	9/7/42	124	27	KIA 17/7/43
108	Bitsch, Ltn Emil	III	5/11/41	108	–	KIA 15/3/44
106	Bauer, Oblt Viktor	III	25/6/41	106	2, EJG 1	S
106	Lucas, Hptm Werner	II	26/7/41	106	–	KIA 24/10/43
102	Lützow, Hptm Günther	I/GS	31/5/40	110	JV 44	KIA 24/4/45
98	Schleef, Uffz Hans	I/III	2/7/41	98	4, 5	KIA 31/12/44
95	Münster, Uffz Leopold	II	26/8/41	95	–	KIA 8/5/44
90	Schentke, Fw Georg	I/III	24/6/41	90	–	MIA 25/12/42
88	von Boremski, Obfw Eberhard	II/III	25/6/41	88	77, EJG 1	S
83	Wessling, Fw Otto	I/III/IV	4/7/41	83	–	KIA 19/4/44
83	Beyer, Oblt Franz	II/III/IV	22/6/41	83	–	KIA 11/2/44
80	Gollob, Hptm Gordon M	II	1/7/41	150	ZG 76, 77	S
77	Grünberg, Fw Hans	II	30/10/42	82	7, JV 44	S
75	Ohlrogge, Fw Walter	II/III	2/7/41	75	–	S
74	Frielinghaus, Ltn Gustav	II/IV	6/10/41	74	EJG 1	S
73	Ewald, Hptm Wolfgang	GS/III	12/6/42	74	52	PoW 14/7/43
71	Fuss, Ltn Hans	II	25/6/41	71	–	DoW 10/11/42

71	Dahl, Oblt Walther	GS, II/III	24/8/41	129	zbV, 300	S
63	Rüffler, Uffz Helmut	I/II/III	23/9/41	88	51	S
60	Kemethmüller, Uffz Heinz	III	19/8/41	89	54, 26	S
58	Schwaiger, Uffz Franz	I/II	3/9/41	58	–	KIA 24/4/44
58	Engfer, Fw Siegfried	III	29/5/42	58	–	S
54	Heckmann, Fw Alfred	II	23/6/41	71	26	S
54	Reiff, Uffz Hans	III	11/7/42	?	?	?
52	Häfner, Ltn Ludwig	I/II	13/6/42	52	–	MIA 10/11/42
52	Ebener, Uffz Kurt	II	24/7/42	57	11	PoW 23/8/44
51	Mertens, Ltn Helmut	GS/I/III	1/11/40	54	LG2, EJG 1	S
51	Dilling, Fw August	GS/I/II	23/6/41	51	–	KIA 14/6/44
51	Michalek, Oblt Georg	I/II	26/7/41	62	54, 108	S
47	Oesau, Hptm Walter	GS/III	24/6/41	127	51, 2, 1	KIA 11/5/44
47	Hübner, Ltn Eckhardt	GS/III	12/7/41	47	–	KIA 28/3/42
46	Daspelgruber, Ltn Franz	I/IV	27/6/42	46	–	MIA 16/7/43
46	Surau, Fw Alfred	III	25/3/43	46	–	DoW 14/10/43
44	Frese, Uffz Hans	II	23/7/42	46	–	S
40	Schütte, Fw Josef	II	24/6/42	40	–	KIA 4/12/43
39	Saborowski, Fw Rudolf	III	29/10/40	39	–	KIA 8/7/42
39	Stolte, Oblt Paul	II	14/3/43	39	1	KIA 18/10/43
38	Sochatzy, Oblt Kurt	III	30/6/41	39	–	PoW 3/8/41
37	Miksch, Uffz Alfred	III	4/9/42	43	1	KIA 1/12/43
37	Ruhl, Ltn Franz	I/II	28/4/43	37	–	KIA 24/12/44
37	Thyben, Uffz Gerhard	II	11/5/43	157	54	S
36	Olejnik, Obfw Robert	I	5/2/41	42	2, 1,400, EJG 2	S
36	Rohwer, Ltn Detlev	I/II	25/6/41	38	1	DOW 30/3/44
36	Löhr, Ltn Ernst-Heinz	I/II	20/8/41	36	–	KIA 22/2/44
36	Zibler, Fw Emil	III	16/9/42	36	–	MIA 5/7/43
36	Weik, Ltn Hans	GS/III/ IV	11/4/43	36	–	S
35	von Einsiedel, Ltn Heinrich *Graf*	III	4/7/42	35	–	PoW 30/8/42
34	Stechmann, Fw Hans	III	15/9/40	?	?	?
33	Schlüter, Fw Harro	I	22/5/42	33	–	KAS 15/4/44
33	Cech, Uffz Franz	II	25/3/43	65	52	?
32	Schuster, Ltn Hermann	II	29/4/43	32	–	KIA 21/7/43
31	Eyrich, Uffz Waldemar	II	17/8/42	31	–	KIA 11/4/44
31	Bringmann, Uffz Arnold	II/IV	23/9/42	?	?	?
30	Langer, Oblt Karl-Heinz	III	24/8/42	30	–	S
30	Schaüble, Fw Karl	III	25/8/42	30	–	KIA 27/2/43
29	Diergardt, Ltn Rolf	III	6/4/42	29	–	MIA 11/8/42
28	Straznicky, Oblt Erwin	I	6/7/42	40	77	MIA 3/10/42
27	Bucholz, Obfw Max	I	17/5/40	28	5, 101, 106	S
27	Kortlepel, Obfw Erwin	II	30/6/41	?	?	?
26	Lüth, Fw Detlev	I	26/6/41	37	1	KIA 6/3/44
26	Koch, Ltn Raimund	III	16/7/43	26	–	KAS 2/11/44
25	Heinzeller, Uffz Josef	II	28/8/40	35	LG 2, 54	?
25	Meckel, Ltn Helmut	I	7/9/40	77		KAS 8/5/43
25	Tichy, Ltn Ekkehard	III/IV	5/7/43	25	53	KIA 16/8/44
25	Wald, Fw Harry	IV	?	25	–	S
24	von Hahn, Hptm Hans	I	10/1/41	34	1, 53, 103	S
24	Baum, Fw Heinz	I	3/9/42	24	–	MIA 12/12/42
24	Giese, Uffz Willy	III	13/9/42	24	–	MIA 31/12/42
24	Zimmermann, Ltn Oskar	II/IV	13/4/44	30	51	S
23	Sannemann, Oblt Heinrich	II	23/6/41	23	–	S
23	Walz, Oblt Albrecht	GS/II	3/7/42	27	–	KIA 11/4/43
23	Dohse, Ltn Hartwig	II	7/5/43	23	–	MIA 31/7/43

Victories with JG 3	Name/Rank	*Gruppe(n)*	Date of Fifth Victory	Total Score	Other JG(s)	Fate
23	Müller, Maj Friedrich-Karl	GS/IV	8/3/44	140	53	KAS 29/5/44
23	Unger, Uffz Willi	IV	19/4/44	23	7	S
23	Maximowitz, Uffz Willi	IV	18/7/44	27	SSt1	MIA 20/4/45
22	Buschmann, Uffz Hubert	I	8/8/42	22	–	KIA 16/8/44
21	Bock, Ltn Eberhard	I	2/9/40	23	1	S
21	Kijewski, Oblt Herbert	II/III	26/6/41	21	1	MIA 16/4/43
21	Vogel, Uffz Wolfgang	II	11/6/42	21	–	MIA 1/8/42
21	Humer, Ltn Alfred	I/IV	10/7/42	21	–	KIA 10/2/44
21	Kaiser, Uffz Theodor	I	20/7/42	?	?	?
21	Lorentzen, Ltn Friedrich	I	26/9/42	21	–	KAS 18/3/43
21	Zimmer, Fw Herbert	III	2/10/42	?	?	?
21	Hofrath, Uffz Kurt	I	3/10/42	21	–	KIA 3/1/43
20	Keller, Oblt Lothar	I/II	21/5/40	20	–	KIA 26/6/41
20	Förg, Fw Rasso	II/IV	30/7/42	20	–	KIA 23/3/44
20	Gosemann, Uffz Heinz	III	19/9/42	20	–	KIA 24/4/44
19	Heesen, Fw Ernst	I	25/6/41	32	1	MIA 3/5/43
19	Gruber, Uffz Otto	I	8/8/42	19	–	KAS 3/4/43
19	Myrrhe, Ltn Lothar	II	9/8/42	19	–	MIA 21/4/43
19	Gerth, Ltn Werner	IV	7/7/44	27	SSt 1	KIA 2/11/44
18	Schmidt, Oblt Winfried	III	26/6/41	19	77	?
18	May, Uffz Heinrich	II	2/7/42	18	–	MIA 22/2/43
18	Roisch, Ltn Kurt	I	6/7/42	?	?	?
18	Wenzel, Oblt Werner	III	5/8/42	18	?	?
18	Mrotzek, Uffz Fritz	I	20/8/42	18	–	KIA 18/12/44
18	Kloss, Fw Werner	II	24/4/43	18	–	KAS 18/10/43
18	Lüdtke, Uffz Horst	II	28/4/43	18	–	KIA 5/6/43
18	Papendick, Uffz Heinz	III	9/7/43	18	–	KIA 2/3/44
18	Hoerschelmann, Ltn, Jürgen	III	14/10/43	18	–	KIA 12/5/44
18	Schäfer, Fw Hans	IV	19/12/43	?	?	?
18	Iffland, Ltn Hans	IV	8/4/44	?	?	S
18	Bösch, Uffz Oskar	IV	18/7/44	18	–	S
18	Drdla, Uffz Hubert	IV	23/12/44	18	7	S
17	Berg, Uffz Rudolf	III	1/7/41	17	–	MIA 28/3/42
17	Krais, Uffz Uwe	I/IV	9/10/42	17	–	KAS 23/7/43
17	Kutz, Obfw Walter	IV	??/4/45	17	–	S
16	Suschko, Fw Leo	I/II	17/8/41	?	?	?
16	Steinicke, Fw Karl-Heinz	II	8/7/42	?	?	?
16	Hagenah, Uffz Walther	I/IV	14/10/42	17	11, 7	S
16	Gräf, Fw Kurt	III	5/7/43	16	–	KAS 25/2/44
16	Romm, Ltn Oskar	I/IV	27/9/44	92	51	S
15	Schiffer, Uffz Johannes	I	8/7/41	15	1	KIA 31/5/42
15	Rüping, Ltn Karl-Emil	III	3/4/43	?	?	?
14	Ehlers, Fw Hans	I	5/2/41	55	1	KIA 27/12/44
14	Faust, Oblt Karl	II	2/7/41	14	–	KAS 12/7/41
14	Raich, Ltn Alfons	I/III	25/7/41	?	1	?
14	Pöske, Uffz Ernst	II	26/7/41	14	–	MIA 22/7/42
14	Reich, Uffz Günther	III	9/9/42	14	–	KIA 2/10/42
14	Dehrmann, Uffz Herbert	II	25/3/43	14	–	KIA 6/8/44
14	Erhardt, Uffz Otto	IV	18/4/44	14	–	KIA 14/1/45
13	Jung, Ltn Hans	III	16/9/42	13	–	PoW 10/11/42
13	Mohn, Uffz Günther	II	10/3/43	?	?	?
13	Traphan, Fw Rudolf	II	31/3/43	13	–	KIA 11/4/44
13	Roller, Obfw Robert	II	6/7/43	13	–	KIA 18/7/44

13	Meyer-Arend, Fw Robert	III	23/2/44	13	–	KIA 27/5/44
13	Loos, Uffz Walter	II/IV	9/4/44	38	300, 301	S
12	Stange, Oblt Willy	I/III	18/8/40	12	–	KAS 22/6/41
12	Bergmann, Ltn Karl	I	2/7/41	12	–	KAS 6/8/42
12	Küpper, Uffz Heinz	I	20/7/41	?	1	?
12	Brenner, Obfw Heinrich	II	17/8/41	12	–	KIA 7/9/41
12	Wirth, Fw Otto	I	8/12/42	12	–	KIA 8/10/43
12	Kutscha, Ltn Herbert	II/IV	25/8/43	47	77, ZG 1, SKG 210, 27, 11	S
12	Florian, Fw Otto	II	8/4/44	12	–	MIA 20/6/44
12	Fritz, Fhj/Fw Hans	I	22/4/44	12	–	KAS 26/11/44
12	Neumann, Uffz Klaus	IV	11/9/44	37	51, 7, JV 44	S
12	Schroer, Maj Werner	GS	15/3/45	114	27, 54	S
11	Neuerburg, Oblt Erwin	III	30/8/40	?	77	?
11	Springer, Fw Herbert	III	9/7/41	?	?	?
11	Rose, Ltn Helmut	I	22/7/42	11	–	PoW 7/10/42
11	Benkendorf, Ltn	I	13/11/42	?	?	?
11	Moritz, Hptm Wilhelm	IV	13/5/44	44	1, 51, 4	S
11	Zink, Ltn Dieter	GS/III/IV	12/5/44	15	–	PoW 11/7/44
11	Löschenkohl, Uffz Ferdinand	IV	15/3/45	11	–	S
11	Bareuther, Ltn Herbert	IV	??/4/45	55	51	MIA 30/4/45
10	Seifert, Uffz Werner	I	8/7/41	?	?	?
10	Setzepfandt, Ltn Karl-Günther	III	6/4/42	?	?	?
10	Bertram, Hptm Karl-Friedrich	I	3/6/42	?	?	?
10	Greisert, Maj Karl-Heinz	III	4/7/42	33	2	KIA 22/7/42
10	Gendelmeyer, Ltn Wolfgang	I	8/7/42	10	–	KIA 1/8/42
10	Willmann, Fw ?	I	10/12/42	?	?	?
10	Fischer, Uffz Alfred	II	22/3/43	10	–	PoW 4/7/43
10	Hanstein, Ltn Helmut	III	5/7/43	?	?	?
10	Stienhans, Uffz Walter	II	12/7/43	10	–	KIA 3/11/43
10	Rentsch, Fw Wolfgang	III	19/12/43	10	7	S
10	Rachner, Ltn Hans	IV	11/4/44	10	–	KIA 7/7/44
10	Jung, Fw Hans-Ulrich	III/IV	8/5/44	10	–	KIA 1/1/45
10	Hoffmann, Uffz Reinhold	IV	30/7/44	?	?	?
10	Angres, Fhj/Fw Heinz	IV	23/8/44	10	–	KIA 16/10/44
9	Kohl, Obfhr ?	II	13/8/41	?	?	?
9	Ponec, Ltn Karlheinz	II	21/8/41	9	–	KAS 13/2/42
9	Pissarski, Uffz Georg	II	15/1/43	?	?	?
9	Seewald, Ltn Karl-Ludwig	II	15/4/43	9	–	KIA 10/10/43
9	Fedgenhäuer, Uffz Martin	II	23/4/43	9	–	KIA 18/7/44
9	Frenzel, Uffz Harald	III	5/7/43	9	–	KIA 22/7/43
9	Stahlberg, Ltn Erwin	III	12/8/43	9	300, 7	KIA 14/4/45
9	Hener, Obfw Rudolf	I	19/2/45	9	–	S
8	von Werra, Oblt Franz	II	28/8/40	21	53	KAS 25/10/41
8	Buddenhagen, Ltn Horst	II	23/6/41	8	–	KIA 25/6/41
8	Beyer, Uffz Horst	II/III	28/6/41	8	–	KIA 11/7/41
8	Winkler, Uffz Ernst	I	7/7/41	15	1	MIA 17/6/43
9	Freitag, Fw Hermann	II	26/7/41	?	?	?
8	Graf, Uffz Egon	III	5/4/42	?	?	?
8	Riha, Ltn Alfred	I	22/7/42	8	–	MIA 28/7/42
8	Weise, Uffz Reinhard	III	14/10/42	8	–	MIA 29/10/42
8	Quaet-Faslem, Oblt Klaus	I	19/12/42	49	LG 2, 53	KAS 30/1/44
8	Schmidt, Ltn Friedrich-Wilhelm	II	17/5/43	8	–	KIA 18/4/44
8	Schaedle, Oblt Gerd	II	2/6/43	?	?	?
8	Schirra, Uffz Helmuth	II	13/7/43	?	?	?
7	Tiedmann, Ltn Helmut	I	7/6/40	7	–	PoW 18/8/40

Victories with JG 3	Name/Rank	*Gruppe(n)*	Date of Fifth Victory	Total Score	Other JG(s)	Fate
7	von Selle, Hptm Erich	II	30/8/40	7	–	S
7	Niedereichholz, Uffz Kurt	I	8/7/41	16	1	MIA 1/1/45
7	Moldenhauer, Oblt Harald	II	17/8/41	9	1	S
7	Helm, Obfhr Albert	II	22/8/41	7	–	KIA 25/5/42
7	Kuhn, Gfr Adalbert	III	20/5/42	7	–	PoW 29/5/42
7	Opalke, Uffz Horst	II	31/5/42	7	–	KAS 20/7/42
7	Brucki, Ltn Edmund	I	28/6/42	?	?	?
7	Schopper, Fw Erich	III	29/7/42	7	–	KIA 15/8/42
7	Burda, Obgefr Johannes	I/IV	7/10/42	7	–	KAS 3/3/44
7	Bornholt, Ltn Wilhelm	I	14/10/42	7	–	DAS 11/4/44
7	Germeroth, Hptm Rudolf	I	28/12/42	7	–	KIA 14/10/43
7	Notemann, Fw Helmut	II	25/1/43	?	?	?
7	Lüdtke, Uffz Heinz	III	6/5/43	7	–	PoW 5/7/43
7	Geyer, Uffz Norbert	III	5/7/43	7	–	KIA 2/7/44
7	Reiser, Ltn Hans	II	5/7/43	7	–	KIA 10/7/43
7	Birnstill, Uffz Franz	III	30/7/43	7	–	KAS 13/2/44
7	Kap-Herr, Oblt Hermann	GS/II/III	4/3/44	7	–	KIA 24/4/44
7	Reinartz, Ltn Fridolin	II	13/4/44	7	–	KIA 6/8/44
7	Nolting, Obfhr Erhard	IV	29/4/44	?	?	?
7	Schmidt, Uffz Karl-Heinz	IV	24/5/44	7	–	MIA 3/8/44
7	Ströbele, Obfw Georg	III	27/5/44	?	?	?
7	Jeworrek, Uffz Heinz	IV	7/7/44	7	–	KIA 20/7/44
7	Hecker, Ltn Karl-Dieter	IV	18/7/44	?	?	?
7	Bauer, Obfw Johann	IV	7/10/44	?	?	?
7	Clässen, Fw Johann	IV	2/11/44	7	–	MIA 25/12/44
7	Müller, Ltn Siegfried	IV	2/12/44	17	SSt 1	S
6	Sprenger, Ltn Gerhard	I	17/5/40	6	–	MIA 16/5/41
6	Keil, Uffz Josef	III	26/8/40	?	302, 301	S
6	Schnabel, Ltn Heinz	I	28/8/40	6	–	PoW 5/9/40
6	Woitke, Oblt Erich	I	18/9/40	29	1	KIA 24/12/44
6	Balthasar, Hptm Wilhelm	I	24/10/40	40	27, 2	KIA 3/7/41
6	Kniewasser, Obfw Hermann	I	12/7/41	6	–	KIA 17/7/41
6	Ressel, Ltn Heinz	I	26/7/41	?	?	?
6	Schiller, Uffz Georg	II	6/7/42	6	–	MIA 9/7/42
6	Matzdorf, Fw Adelmar	III	2/10/42	6	–	MIA 26/10/42
6	Blaut, Uffz Heinrich	I	29/11/42	6	–	PoW 8/12/42
6	Boll, Uffz Hermann	III	11/12/42	6	–	MIA 12/12/42
6	Fisher, Ltn Max-Bruno	II	5/7/43	?	?	?
6	Bohatsch, Ltn Walter	II	7/7/43	16	7	S
6	Schmied, Ltn Hermann	IV	17/9/43	6	–	KIA 10/2/44
6	Dräger, Fw Paul	II	4/10/43	?	?	?
6	Reinwald, Oblt ?	III	25/2/44	?	?	?
6	Ostrowitzki, Uffz Bruno	I	11/4/44	?	?	?
6	Schulz, Uffz Egon	IV	13/4/44	?	?	?
6	Clemens, Uffz Curt	III	12/5/44	6	–	KIA 27/1/45
6	Franz, Ltn Richard	IV	12/5/44	?	?	?
6	Jäger, Uffz ?	II	28/5/44	?	?	?
6	Wielebinski, Fw Paul	III	21/6/44	6	–	KIA 25/6/44
6	Scholz, Uffz Hans-Joachim	IV	29/7/44	6	–	KIA 3/8/44
6	Vivroux, Uffz Gerhard	IV	27/9/44	11	SSt 1	DoW 25/10/44
6	Keune, Uffz Helmut	IV	23/12/44	6	–	KIA 14/1/45
6	Claussen, Fw ?	III	11/3/45	?	?	?
6	Raab, Uffz ?	IV	??/4/45	6	–	MIA 1/5/45

	Name/Rank	Gruppe(n)	Date		Other JG(s)	Fate
5	Landry, Ltn Hans-Herbert	I	18/8/40	5	–	DoW 23/9/40
5	Achleitner, Ltn Franz	III	20/8/40	5	–	PoW 24/8/40
5	Göttmann, Ltn Leonhard	III	24/8/40	?	?	?
5	Westerhoff, Oblt Karl	II	26/8/40	?	?	?
5	Götz, Obfw Horst	II	15/9/40	5	–	KAS 29/10/40
5	Troha, Oblt Erwin	III	26/10/40	5	–	PoW 29/10/40
5	Jaksch, Uffz ?	I	29/6/41	?	?	?
5	Schulz, Uffz Günther	I	12/7/41	5	–	KIA 31/7/41
5	Borchers, Oblt Hans-Jürgen	I	16/7/41	?	?	?
5	Eichler, Ltn Kurt	I	17/7/41	?	?	?
5	Schönfedlt, Oblt Heinz	II	8/8/41	?	?	?
5	Andres, Hptm Werner	III	25/8/41	?	–	S
5	Wallrath, Uffz Karlheinz	III	3/10/41	5	–	KIA 13/2/42
5	Ehmke, Uffz Otto	III	26/2/42	5	–	KAS 23/5/42
5	Kirsten, Uffz Otto	III	6/7/42	?	?	?
5	von Cramon, Hptm Friedrich-Franz	GS/I	23/7/42	5	–	PoW 1/8/42
5	Krug, Fw Willi	I	1/10/42	?	?	?
5	Loos, Uffz Gottfried	III	9/10/42	5	–	MIA 25/10/42
5	Springer, Obfw Herbert	I	16/10/42	?	?	?
5	Teegler, Fw Werner	I	23/10/42	5	–	MIA 4/11/42
5	Rose, Uffz Werner	III	14/11/42	5	–	MIA 14/11/42
5	Obst, Uffz Heinz	I	10/12/42	5	–	MIA 3/1/43
5	Kühnel, Fw Hans	II	25/3/43	?	?	?
5	Löffler, Uffz Oskar	III	31/3/43	5	–	KIA 7/5/43
5	Hinz, Uffz ?	III	19/12/43	?	?	?
5	Pintsch, Uffz Rudolf	IV	3/3/44	5	–	KIA 3/3/44
5	Hinkelmann, Oblt Joachim	I	22/4/44	5	–	24/4/44
5	Pankalla, Uffz Gerhard	III	24/4/44	5	–	KIA 11/7/44
5	Zehart, Oblt Otmar	IV	8/5/44	?	?	?
5	Metz, Ltn Rudolf	IV	12/5/44	?	?	?
5	Hoyer, Ltn Johannes	II	30/6/44	?	?	?
5	Brandt, Fw Josef	IV	18/7/44	?	?	?
5	Heinig, Uffz Günther	IV	22/8/44	5	–	KIA 24/8/44
5	Wichmann, Fw Helmut	IV	12/9/44	5	–	KIA 23/12/44
5	Haase, Oblt Horst	IV	28/9/44	56	51	KIA 26/11/44
5	Küttner, Oblt Siegfried	IV	2/11/44	5	–	MIA 1/5/45
5	Kosse, Hptm Wolfgang	IV	24/12/44	28	5, 26	MIA 24/12/44
5	Glaubig, Ltn Gotthard	IV	27/12/44	12	–	KIA 27/12/44
5	Brandt, Ltn Walther	I	3/3/45	42	51	S
5	Angst, Ltn Paul	III	24/4/45	5	–	S

Notes and Abbreviations

(*) Lists all known aces (five or more victories) but may not be complete due to lack of information relating to closing months of war

Name/Rank: rank shown as at time of fifth victory

Gruppe(n): indicates those with which the ace is known to have served within the *Geschwader* (not necessarily shown in chronological order).

'GS' signifies service with the *Geschwaderstab*

Other JG(s): refers to units (excluding training schools) that the ace is known to have served with during his operational career. A dash signifies that he served solely with JG 3. A question mark indicates 'not known'

Abbreviations as follows;

EJG - *Ergänzungsjagdgeschwader*
JV - *Jagdverband*
LG - *Lehrgeschwader*
SKG - *Schnellkampfgeschwader*
SSt - *Sturmstaffel*
zbV - 'Special duties' *Geschwader*
ZG - *Zerstörergeschwader*

Fate: Abbreviations as follows;
KIA - killed in action
MIA - missing in action
KAS - killed on active service
DAS - died on active service
DoW - died of wounds
PoW - prisoner-of-war
S - known to have survived war

COLOUR PLATES

1
Bf 109E-4 'Black Chevron and Triangle' of Hauptmann Günther Lützow, *Gruppenkommandeur* I./JG 3, Hargimont, Belgium, May 1940

Apart from the green *Tatzelwurm*, or dragon, emblem of the *Gruppenstab* I./JG 3 worn on its cowling, this machine is in otherwise standard early-1940 finish and markings. The modest trio of kills displayed on the rudder – the last of them for a French Curtiss Hawk downed southeast of Charleroi shortly after midday on 15 May 1940 – offer little indication of the illustrious career ahead for the pilot of this machine.

2
Bf 109E-4 'Black Chevron' of Leutnant Egon Troha, *Gruppen-Adjutant* III./JG 3, St Trond, Belgium, May 1940

The only obvious difference between this *Emil* and the one immediately above it is the *Gruppe* badge – III./JG 3's chosen motif was a large spear-wielding wasp (?), applied beneath the cockpit. The single victory bar is for a Dutch Fokker C.V despatched south of Waalhaven on 10 May 1940, the opening day of the *Blitzkrieg* in the west. It was a 'first' for Egon Troha, and the second (after Massmann's Fokker D.XXI kill) for the *Geschwader*.

3
Bf 109E-4 'Black Chevron and Triangle' of Hauptmann Günther Lützow, *Gruppenkommandeur* I./JG 3, Berneuil, France, June 1940

What a difference a month makes! The *Kommandeur's* machine has been completely transformed by the application of large blotches of camouflage colour to its cowling and sides. The *Stab* symbol has also undergone radical revision, the previously small inner triangle having been enlarged to equal the size of, and be positioned *behind*, the chevron. Note, too, the number of victory markings, which have now grown to seven.

4
Bf 109E-1 'Black 5' of Leutnant Franz Beyer, 8./JG 3, Desvres, France, September 1940

'Black 5', the mount of future 83-victory ace Leutnant Franz Beyer, displays the typical Battle of Britain-period markings associated with III./JG 3, including the yellow cowling extending in a slight curve diagonally back to the base of the windscreen, and all-yellow rudder. Note also the *Gruppe's* new badge, the two-bladed battleaxe, which has already supplanted the spear-toting wasp.

5
Bf 109E-4 'Black Chevron and Circle' of Leutnant Detlev Rohwer, *Gruppen-TO* I./JG 3, Colombert, France, September 1940

Flown by future Knight's Cross winner Leutnant Detlev Rohwer, then the Technical (i.e. Engineering) Officer of I./JG 3, this *Emil* sports a variation on the yellow tactical markings carried by most Luftwaffe fighters during the Battle of Britain. Here, the washable yellow paint applied to the nose follows the line of the cowling panels (and completely obliterates the *Gruppenstab's* green *Tatzelwurm*).

6
Bf 109E-4 'Black 1' of Oberleutnant Herbert Kijewski, *Staffelkapitän* 5./JG 3, Wierre-au-Bois, France, September 1940

Proving that there are exceptions to every rule, Herbert Kijewski's machine wears no yellow markings at all other than the metal *Staffelkapitän's* pennant attached to the aerial mast. Note II. *Gruppe's* black and white gyronny shield carried below the cockpit, and the name *Erika* on the cowling. The last of the three kill bars at the base of the tailfin is for Oberleutnant Kijewski's only Battle of Britain victory – a Hurricane (of No 73 Sqn?) downed over the Essex coast on 5 September.

7
Bf 109E-4 'Black 6' of Unteroffizier Alfred Heckmann, 5./JG 3, Arques, France, September 1940

'Fred' Heckmann, who ended the war with 71 kills and a posting to the Me 262-equipped JV 44 (which he failed to reach before the German surrender), had begun it as a founder member of 5./JG 3. Like his *Staffelkapitän* Herbert Kijewski (above), he too had three victories by the close of the Battle of Britain. In his case, however, the ratio was reversed – one over France and two (both Spitfires) over England.

8
Bf 109E-4 'White 11' of Leutnant Alfons Raich, 7./JG 3, Desvres, France, September 1940

Alfons Raich's 'White 11' is seen here in what can only be described as a state of transition. Although the nose (including spinner) has been given a coat of yellow paint, the rudder remains untouched. Nor is the new III. *Gruppe* badge – reportedly introduced in September 1940 – anywhere in evidence. Instead, the cowling bears the personal marking *Herzi* ('Sweetie') and a much simplified rendering of the earlier 'Belligerent wasp'. Leutnant Raich was to claim 14 victories with JG 3, but details of his subsequent career, including a period of service with JG 1, are sketchy.

9
Bf 109E-7 'Black 1' of Leutnant Helmut Meckel, *Staffelkapitän* 2./JG 3, St Omer-Wizernes, France, October 1940

Leutnant Meckel's first nine victories (see rudder tally) were all scored during the Battle of Britain. He would take that total to 25 before ill health forced him to retire from flying duties in mid-July 1941. It is not known how many, if any, further kills he achieved after returning to active service as the *Geschwader* Ia (Operations Officer) of JG 77 the following year. Note that although 2./JG 3's individual aircraft numerals are black, the *Gruppe Tatzelwurm* is in the 'official' *Staffel* colour of red.

10
Bf 109E-4 'Yellow 5' of Oberleutnant Egon Troha, *Staffelkapitän* 9./JG 3, Desvres, France, October 1940

After serving as the Adjutant of III. *Gruppe* (and gaining four kills while so doing), Egon Troha was appointed *Kapitän* of 9. *Staffel* on 1 October 1940. He added one further victory, a Hurricane on 26 October, before forced-landing in Kent three days later. His 'Yellow 5' bears a wealth of markings, including the *Gruppe* badge on the port side of the nose (and the name *Erika* – clearly a popular girl! – on the starboard), plus 9. *Staffel's* seahorse emblem below the cockpit. All five of Troha's kills are shown on the rudder, although the significance of the top hat separating Nos 2 and 3 can only be guessed at – perhaps to differentiate between the two victories claimed against the French and the three scored against the British, whom many Germans referred to dismissively as the 'Lords'?

11
Bf 109F-2 'Yellow 1' of Oberleutnant Heinrich Sannemann, *Staffelkapitän* 6./JG 3, Monchy-Breton, France, May 1941
Depicted during II./JG 3's brief return to the Channel front in May 1941, this new F-2 wears the finish and markings typical of the period. Heinrich Sannemann had just three victories to his name at this time. Before the war ended he would add 20 more, all scored with II. *Gruppe* between lengthy spells of instructing at various training establishments.

12
Bf 109F-2 'White 7' of Oberleutnant Robert Olejnik, *Staffelkapitän* 1./JG 3, Luzk, Poland, July 1941
Robert Olejnik's 'White 7' typifies the changes made when JG 3 moved from the Channel front to the eastern front. A fresh coat of camouflage paint has been applied to the earlier all-yellow cowling (leaving just the lower panel in its former colour) and rudder, and a new eastern theatre yellow fuselage band has been added immediately aft of the fuselage cross. 1. *Staffel's* white *Tatzelwurm* has survived the changes, but note too the white bar on the rudder scoreboard denoting Olejnik's 20th kill. In the past this was the 'magic number' that had practically guaranteed a pilot the Knight's Cross, but not in Russia. Oberleutnant Olejnik would have to add another 11 victories to the 21 shown here, and wait a further three weeks, before being decorated on 27 July.

13
Bf 109F-2 'Yellow 7' of Oberleutnant Viktor Bauer, *Staffelkapitän* 9./JG 3, Polonoye, USSR, July 1941
Wearing a similar finish to the machine above, Viktor Bauer's 'Yellow 7' displays an even more impressive rudder scoreboard – four aircraft destroyed on the ground (top row), plus 34 aerial victories (the last three a trio of DB-3s all brought down on 13 July). Note that, unlike I. *Gruppe*, most of III./JG 3's machines carried the yellow theatre band at the rear of the fuselage in order to accommodate the III. *Gruppe* vertical bar aft of the cross.

14
Bf 109F-2 'Yellow 6' of Leutnant Helmut Mertens, 9./JG 3, Belaya-Zerkov, USSR, August 1941
There had to be exceptions, of course, and with its *Gruppe* bar superimposed on a yellow band immediately behind the fuselage cross, 'Pitt' Mertens' 'Yellow 6' was clearly one of them. Note also what appears to be a replacement, or heavily overpainted, engine cowling and signs of previous ownership beneath the individual aircraft number. A member of the original pre-war I.(J)/LG 2, Mertens was one of seven JG 3 pilots who would be awarded the Knight's Cross for reaching 50 victories during the latter half of 1942.

15
Bf 109F-4 'Black Chevron and Triangle' of Hauptmann Gordon M Gollob, *Gruppenkommandeur* II./JG 3, Mironovka, USSR, September 1941
Just ten days and five kills away from his Knight's Cross (awarded on 18 September for 42 victories), future *General der Jagdflieger* Gordon M Gollob has kept a careful record of his successes to date, starting with the first victory claimed during the Polish campaign as a member of I./ZG 76. Gollob would be the first fighter pilot ever to claim 150 victories, 80 of which had been achieved while serving with II./JG 3.

16
Bf 109F-4/trop 'Black Chevron and Bar' of Leutnant Max-Bruno Fischer, *Gruppen*-Adjutant II./JG 3 'Udet', Sciacca, Sicily, February 1942
As the only *Gruppe* of the newly titled JG 3 'Udet' to see service in the Mediterranean area, many of II./JG 3's tropicalised F-4s wore the standard 'Africa' camouflage of overall desert tan uppersurfaces combined with light blue undersides, plus white aft fuselage theatre band (and wingtips). As well as retaining the II. *Gruppe* badge, Leutnant Fischer's machine also displays his personal emblem – an unidentified cartoon-like figure (of a mouse carrying a sack and umbrella?), the significance of which is no longer known.

17
Bf 109F-4/Z 'Yellow 4' of Oberfeldwebel Eberhard von Boremski, 9./JG 3 'Udet', Soltsy, USSR, February 1942
No hint of sun or sand here, just a workmanlike winter finish much more suited to the weather conditions on the Russian front early in 1942. With his score currently in the high twenties, Eberhard von Boremski would survive the war with a final total of 88, all claimed while flying with JG 3.

18
Bf 109F-4/trop 'White 1' of Oberleutnant Walther Dahl, *Staffelkapitän* 4./JG 3 'Udet', San Pietro, Sicily, March 1942
Back to warmer climes with this desert-finished 'White 1', the mount of *Staffelkapitän* Oberleutnant Walther Dahl. Although the current 17-victory Dahl was not among the claimants for the five confirmed kills credited to II. *Gruppe* during its brief period of service in the Mediterranean, he was later to find fame as one of the leading exponents of *Sturm* operations, amassing a final total of 129 enemy aircraft destroyed by war's end.

19
Bf 109F-4/trop 'Yellow 4' of Obergefreiter Walther Hagenah, 3./JG 3 'Udet', Wiesbaden-Erbenheim, Germany, April 1942
When the new I./JG 3 'Udet' was formed in March 1942 it was clearly equipped with machines originally destined for the Mediterranean theatre. To make them more suitable for service in Russia, large segments of green and grey paint were added to their 'desert' finish to produce this striking camouflage scheme. Note also the new 'crossed-swords' *Gruppe* badge. Walther Hagenah, whose first victory would be a LaGG-3 downed on 12 August 1942, also later served as a *Sturm* pilot, before ending the war flying Me 262 jets with JG 7.

20
Bf 109F-4/trop 'Black Chevron and Triangle' of Hauptmann Kurt Brändle, *Gruppenkommandeur* II./JG 3 'Udet', Mariyevka, USSR, July 1942

Although its supercharger air intake filter has been removed, this machine is also an F-4/trop. Bearing the tell-tale signs of a previous identity (overpainting around the *Kommandeur* markings), it saw brief service as the mount of Hauptmann Brändle during the first half of July 1942. Having been awarded the Knight's Cross on 1 July for 49 victories, that tally had risen to 63 by the middle of the month. Brändle would ultimately claim 137 victories (from a final tally of 172) during his service with JG 3, making him the *Geschwader's* second-highest scorer.

21
Bf 109F-4 'Black Chevron and Circle' of Leutnant Heinrich *Graf* von Einsiedel, *Gruppen*-Adjutant III./JG 3 'Udet', Millerovo, USSR, July 1942

Appearing here for the first time is the new 'winged U' *Geschwader* emblem adopted by JG 3 upon being given the honour title 'Udet'. Also adorning this F-4 are the III. *Gruppe* 'battleaxe' badge and the *Stab* insignia of an adjutant. But, for some reason, there is no *Gruppe* vertical bar aft of the fuselage cross. The last of the eight victory bars seen on the rudder is for an Il-2 *Shturmovik* brought down on 16 July – the day after III. *Gruppe's* arrival at Millerovo.

22
Bf 109G-2 'Black Chevron and Bars' of Major Wolf-Dietrich Wilcke, *Geschwaderkommodore* JG 3 'Udet', Morosovskaya-West, USSR, December 1942

One of at least two G-2s available to the *Kommodore* towards the end of 1942 as the Battle of Stalingrad was approaching its climax, this particular aircraft was a so-called *'Kanonenboot'* (or 'gunboat') – i.e. it had an additional pair of 20 mm cannon in underwing gondolas. Although no victory markings are displayed, 'Fürst' Wilcke was to claim 15 Red Air Force machines in the Stalingrad area during December 1942, taking his overall total to 155 by the close of the year.

23
Bf 109G-2 'Black 1' of Leutnant Joachim Kirschner, *Staffelkapitän* 5./JG 3 'Udet, Morosovskaya-South, USSR, December 1942

More suitably attired for the harsh wintry conditions raging on the Stalingrad front in the final weeks of 1942, this is the machine of Leutnant Joachim Kirschner, who had just been awarded the Knight's Cross (for his 51st victory, a LaGG-3 downed on 29 October). He was to become JG 3's highest scorer of all, taking his total of enemy aircraft destroyed to 175 before being posted away to become the *Gruppenkommandeur* of IV./JG 27 in October 1943.

24
Bf 109G-4 'Black 7' of Oberleutnant Detlev Rohwer, *Staffelkapitän* 2./JG 3 'Udet', München-Gladbach, Germany, May 1943

Leutnant Rohwer was the Technical Officer of the original I./JG 3 prior to that unit's redesignation as II./JG 1 in January 1942. There, he served as both *Staffelkapitän* of 6./JG 1 and acting-*Kommandeur*, before returning to JG 3 to replace the missing Oberleutnant Erwin Straznicky as *Staffelkapitän* of the 'new' 2./JG 3 'Udet' on 4 October 1942. Throughout it all there was one constant – Rohwer's personal emblem. Carried on all his machines, and seen here on his G-4 *Kanonenboot*, it portrays the medieval German knight-adventurer Götz von Berlichingen in typical pose, inviting his enemies to 'kiss my arse!'.

25
Bf 109G-6/trop 'Black 11' of Feldwebel Hans Kühnel, 11./JG 3 'Udet', San Severo, Italy, August 1943

When first formed, IV./JG 3 'Udet' was equipped with G-6/trops for service in Italy. Intended primarily for the anti-bomber role, its machines carried additional underwing armament – either 20 mm cannon or 210 mm rockets (as shown here on Kühnel's 'Black 11'). Note the spiral spinner and the odd combination of yellow lower cowling and wingtips with a white Mediterranean theatre band around the rear fuselage. Note too the small 'winged U' *Geschwader* badge ahead of the filter intake, and the 'wavy bar' IV. *Gruppe* marking.

26
Bf 109G-6y 'Yellow 6' of Oberfeldwebel Alfred Surau, 9./JG 3 'Udet', Bad Wörishofen, Germany, September 1943

The most distinctive feature of this G-6y *Kanonenboot* is the 'eye' – 9. *Staffel's* striking insignia – painted on the *'Beule'*, or bulge, of the ammunition feed fairing. But note too the 43 kill markings on the rudder. The first of Alfred Surau's 41 eastern front victories had been a Soviet fighter downed on 28 February 1943. During Defence of the Reich operations he would add five B-17s, only to succumb to wounds received while attacking the last of them on 14 October 1943.

27
Bf 109G-6y 'White 5' of Leutnant Erwin Stahlberg, acting-*Staffelkapitän* 7./JG 3 'Udet', Bad Wörishofen, Germany, October 1943

This *Kanonenboot*, the mount of Leutnant Erwin Stahlberg, utilises the *'Beule'* to display 7. *Staffel's* even more visually striking insignia – a large white comet. Note also III./JG 3's practice at this time of applying the *Gruppe* vertical bar in black, irrespective of the individual *Staffel* colour. Unlike the unfortunate Alfred Surau (above), who died of his wounds on the day of his 46th, and final, victory, Erwin Stahlberg was to survive for another 18 months. Twice wounded early in 1944, he claimed his ninth, and last, recorded victory with JG 3 on 27 June of that year. He subsequently served with both JGs 300 and 7, but is not known to have scored any further kills before his Me 262 was shot down by P-51s on 14 April 1945.

28
Bf 109G-5 'Black 6' of Leutnant Walter Bohatsch, 5./JG 3 'Udet', Schiphol, the Netherlands, November 1943

In common with all II. *Gruppe* machines of the late 1943 period, this heavily dappled G-5 eschews all tactical and theatre markings, the emphasis now being solely on camouflage. But note II./JG 3's peculiar practice at this time of displaying the *Geschwader's* 'winged U' in mirror image (i.e. facing backwards) and adding a large red dot beneath it. The reason for this latter, which first appeared on the Russian front (see profile 23), is no longer known.

29
Bf 109G-6/AS 'Black 7' of Leutnant Walter Bohatsch, acting-*Staffelkapitän* 2./JG 3 'Udet', Burg bei Magdeburg, Germany, May 1944

In April 1944 Walter Bohatsch (see previous profile) was transferred briefly to I./JG 3 as acting-*Staffelkapitän* in place of the fallen Leutnant Harro Schlüter, who had been killed while carrying out a dummy attack on a Ju 88 during I. *Gruppe's* training as a specialised high-altitude anti-bomber unit. In May 1944 I./JG 3 'Udet' received its first G-6/AS fighters in the new all-grey high-altitude scheme shown here. Details of Bohatsch's career after returning to 5./JG 3 in the summer of 1944 are sketchy, but he claimed his last three victories of the war while flying Me 262s with JG 7.

30
Fw 190A-8/R-2 'Black 14' of Unteroffizier Oskar Bösch, 14.(*Sturm*)/JG 3 'Udet', Schafstädt, Germany, October 1944

IV. *Gruppe* had returned from Italy (see profile 25) in the late summer of 1943 to retrain as a Defence of the Reich unit. In the spring of 1944 it then converted from its Bf 109s onto Fw 190s to become the Luftwaffe's first dedicated *Sturmgruppe*. Initially, its Focke-Wulfs boasted all-black cowlings, together with the *Geschwader's* white Defence of the Reich bands and IV. *Gruppe* 'wavy bar' markings. By the autumn of 1944, however, these had all disappeared, and IV.(*Sturm*)/JG 3's machines were garbed in the same anonymous finish as 18-victory Oskar Bösch's 'Black 14' shown here.

31
Bf 109K-4 'Black Chevron and Triangle' of Major Karl-Heinz Langer, *Gruppenkommandeur* III./JG 3 'Udet', Pasewalk, Germany, April 1945

As the war entered its final few weeks, the pilots of JG 3 'Udet' – aces and tyros alike – were flying some of the most advanced piston-engined single-seat fighters to come out of Germany's battered aircraft factories. Photographs from these last chaotic days are rare, but this reconstruction based on all available references depicts the machine of Karl-Heinz Langer, all 30 of whose victories were achieved during his four years of service with III. *Gruppe*.

32
Fw 190D-9 'Green 7' of Feldwebel Hubert Drdla, 13.(*Sturm*)/JG 3 'Udet', Prenzlau, Germany, April 1945

Photographs of IV. *Gruppe's* final complement of Fw 190D-9 'Long-noses' are likewise limited to a well-known and oft-published few. This is, therefore, of necessity another reconstruction (based on logbook entries and other known data) of the machine flown by Hubert Drdla shortly before his transfer to JG 7 as the war neared its close. Drdla claimed no kills on the Me 262, all 18 of his recorded victories (six against the Western allies and twelve in the east) having been gained as a member of IV.(*Sturm*)/JG 3 'Udet'.

INDEX

Numbers in bold refer to illustrations and captions. All aircraft are German unless otherwise stated.

100-victory ban 31, 40, **42**, 43

ace status 8–9, 27, 60, 63, 69, 83
    centurions 48, 50, 61, 65, 70, 71, **80**, 82
    semi-centurions 25, **36**, **36**, 37, **40**, 41, **41**, 43, 44, **46**, 47, 48, 49, 50, 71, 75
Achleitner, Leutnant Franz 14–15, 16
aircraft
    B-24 Liberator bomber (US) 65, 74, 76
    B-26 Marauder bomber (US) 61, **77**, 78
    Boeing B-17 bomber (US) 59, 60, **61**, 62, 63, 64, 66, 75, 76, 79
    Bristol Beaufighter fighter (British) **60**, 60–61
    Bristol Blenheim IV bomber (British) 10–11, 12, 13, 20, 21
    Focke-Wulf Fw 190 fighter **58**, 66–67, 71, 76, 78, 83
    Hurricane fighter (British) 14, 18, 19, 21, 34
    Ilyushin DB-3 bomber (USSR) 25, **26**, 30, 31, **46**
    Ilyushin Il-2 *Shturmovik* ground attack plane (USSR) 39, 43, 45, 48, 49, 50
    LaGG-3 fighter (USSR) 39, 46, 48
    Messerschmitt Bf 109E 'Emil' fighter 10, 13, 15, 16, 18, **51–53**
    Messerschmitt Bf 109F-4/trops fighter 32, 33, **33, 34, 54, 55**
    Messerschmitt Bf 109F 'Friedrich' fighter 21, 23, **29**, 32, **53–54, 55, 56**
    Messerschmitt Bf 109G fighter **56–58, 63,** 66–67
    MiG-3 fighter (USSR) 31, 39, 49
    P-38 Lightning fighter (US) 65, 66
    P-47 Thunderbolt fighter-bomber (US) 60, 61, 63, 65, 78

P-51 Mustang fighter (US) 66, 69, 74, 76
Petlyakov Pe-2 fighter (USSR) 27, 30, 41, 42, 49, 82, 83
Polikarpov I-16 fighter (USSR) 23, 27, 36
Supermarine Spitfire fighter (British) 14, 17, 19, 21, 48, **61**, 65, 69, 81, 84
Tupolev SB bomber (USSR) 24, 25, 30
Typhoon fighter-bomber (British) 79, 80, 81
Yakovlev Yak-1 fighter (USSR) 41, 44, 50
Yakovlev Yak-4 bomber (USSR) **36**, 37
aircraft recognition for kill claims 34, 76
airlift of supplies to Demyansk pocket 36–37
Allied landings in Normandy 67, 68
Ardennes offensive, the 78–80, **79**
arrival of IV./JG 3 63

Balthasar, Hauptmann Wilhelm 17, **17**, 19
Bär, Major Heinz 71, **71, 80**, 81, 82
Bareuther, Leutnant Herbert 84
Battle of Britain, the 13–21
Battle of Kiev, the 30, 42
'Battle of Oschersleben', the 74–75
Battle of the Bulge, the 78–80, **79**
Battleaxe, JG 3 *Gruppe* badge **19**
Bauer, Feldwebel Josef 16, 18
Bauer, Oberleutnant Viktor 25, **25**, 26, 37, **37, 38, 42**, 43
BEF (British Expeditionary Force) 11
Beikiefer, Unteroffizier Michael 34
Beyer, Major Franz 14, 24, 28, **36–37**, 37, 49, 50, 63, 65
Bitsch, Hauptmann Emil 30, 49, 50, 62, 65
Blitzkrieg 8, 11–12, 17, **17**
Boremski, Oberfeldwebel Eberhard von 37, **37, 38**, 43, **49**
Bösch, Feldwebel Oskar 81, 83

Brändle, *Gruppenkommandeur* Major Kurt 35, 38, **40**, 40–41, 48, 49–50, 61, 62
Brandt, Leutnant Walter 78, 82
Bucholz, Oberfeldwebel Max 10, 28, **28**

casualties 27, 29, 35, 36–37, 38, 42, 43–44, 46–47, 50, 61, 64–66, **65, 66**, 67, 68, 69, 76, 77, 79, 81, 82–83
Chuikov, Lt-Gen V I 42–43, 47
combat fatigue 67
command changes 19, 40
conferring of decoration criteria 29–30
Crimean front, the 30–31

Dahl, Major Walther 24, 27, **35**, 40, 59, 60, 62, **62**, 65
Daspelgruber, Leutnant Franz 46, 64
Defence of the Reich operations 59–68, 72–81
difference between western and eastern fronts 63
Dilling, Oberfeldwebel Gustav 45, 48, 71
Drdla, Feldwebel Hubert 78, 83

Ebener, Feldwebel Kurt **46**
Ehlers, Feldwebel Hans 20, **20**, 28
Eighth Air Force (Allied) 78, 79
enemy aircraft downed 12
Engfer, Feldwebel Siegfried 43, **43**
Ettel, Leutnant Wolf 41, 48
Ewald, Major Wolfgang 44, **47**, 50
Experten 22, 36, 39, 43, 48, 49, 61, 64

Fall Rot (Case Red) 11–12
freie Jagd sweeps 24, 26, 37, 78
Frielinghaus, Hauptmann Gustav 64, 65
Fuss, Leutnant Hans 24, 41, 44

INDEX

Gembloux raid by RAF 10–11, 13
Gollob, Hauptmann Gordon M. 21, 24, 29, 31, **31**, 33
Göring, Hermann 15, 32, 45
Göttmann, Leutnant Leonhard 16, 18
Greim, *General der Flieger* Robert Ritter von 22
Greisert, Major Karl-Heinz 38, 42, **42**, 44
Grünberg, Leutnant Hans 50, **50**, 68–69

Haase, Hauptmann Horst 75, 77
Hahn, Hauptmann Hans von 4, 15, **15**, 20, 25, 26, 26, 28, **29**
Hecker, Leutnant Karl-Dieter **82**
Heckmann, Unteroffiziere Alfred 14, 29, 41
Heinzeller, Josef **7**
Hitler, Adolf **7**, 45, 49, 78, 81
Hoerschelmann, Leutnant Jürgen 62, 67
Hübner, Leutnant Eckhardt 31, 37

Ibel, Oberstleutnant Max 6, 7
insignia 4, **15**, **19**, **29**, 32, **39**, **40**, **51–58**, 63

Kap-herr, Oberleutnant Hermann *Freiherr* 60, 66
Keller, Hauptmann Lothar 11, 12, 19, 24
Kemethmüller, Feldwebel Heinz 43, **43**
Keune, Unteroffizier Helmut 78, 81
Kienitz, Hauptmann Walter 7, 8, 17
kill rates 37, 38–39, **40**, 40–41, **42**, 43, 45–46, 48, 49, 59, **71**, 73–74, 83, 84
  in Operation *Barbarossa* 22, 24, 25, 26, **26**, 29, **34**
Kirschner, Leutnant Joachim 34, 41, 44, 47, 48, 49–50, **50**, 61, **61**
Knight's Cross, the 9, **20**, **21**, 22, 24, 26, 28, 29, 31, 37, **37**, 41, **43**, 47, 65, **65**, 70, 77
Koall, Hauptmann Gerhard 83
Koch, Oberleutnant Raimund 69, **70**
Kosse, Hauptmann Wolfgang **79**, 80
Krahl, Hauptmann Karl-Heinz 33, 34, 35
Kursk tank battle 49
Kutscha, Leutnant Herbert **63**, 64

Langer, Hauptmann Karl-Heinz 46, 69, **71**, 77, 78, 83
Lemke, Hauptmann Wilhelm 43, 49, 60, 61, 62
Lucas, Oberleutnant Werner 29, **41**, 50, 61
Luftwaffe, the
  I./(J)/LG (*Lehrgeschwader*) 2 6
  I./ZG (*Zerstörer*) 2 (I./JG 231) 6
  II. *Fliegerkorps* 32
  JG 1
    II./JG 1 (I./JG 3) 28
  JG 2 'Richthofen' 26, 33, 38, **42**
  JG 3 'Udet' 7, 8, 9, 12, 14, 16, 17, 18, 19, **19**, 19–20, 21, **22**, 23, 24, 36
    I./JG 3 38, 39, 45, 46, 47, 59, 60, 61, 63, 68, 72, 76–77, 78, 81, 82
      1./JG 3 **41**, 46, **53**, 60, 65, 66, **66**
      2./JG 3 45, 46, **46**, **53**, **56**, **58**, 66, 76, 78, 82
      3./JG 3 44, 46, 47, **55**, 62, 63, 64, 66, 71
    I./JG 3 (II./JG 1) 6–7, 8, **8**, **9**, 9–11, 12, 13, 17, 20, 21, 23, 24, 27, 28, **29**
      1./JG 3 10, 11, 12, 19, **23**
      2./JG 3 20, **21**, **25**, **28**
      3./JG 3 17
    II./JG 3 **8**, 12, 14, 17, 19, 21, **21**, 24, 25, 27, 29, 30, 31, 32, 33–34, **34**, 35, 40–41, 45, 46, 47–48, 61, 68–69, 72, 77, 82
      4./JG 3 21, 24, 31, 34, **35**, 38, 41, **41**, 48, 50, 60, 61, 68, 78, 81
      5./JG 3 35, 41, 48, 49–50, **50**, 61, 67, 68
      6./JG 3 19, 30, 34, 35, **35**, 41, 44, 48, 61, 77
    III./JG 3 7, 8, 9, 12, 14, 16, 17, 18, 19, **19**, 21, **21**, 25–26, 29, 30, 33, 36, 37, 42, 43,

45, 47–49, 59–60, **62**, 63, 65, 68, 69, **70**, 72, 82–83
      7./JG 3 28, **28**, 37, 49, 59, **62**, 64, 69
      8./JG 3 14, 23, 30, **36**, 36–37, 42, 49, 50, 62, 69, 70
      9./JG 3 14–15, **25**, 26, **27**, **37**, 38, **38**, 43, 49, 60, 62, **62**, 66, 70, **74**, 77, 78, 81
    IV.(*Sturm*)/JG 3 49, 63, **63**, 64–65, 66, 67, 71, 72–73, **73**, 74, 75, 81, 83
      10./JG 3 (16.(*Sturm*)/Jg 3) 63–64, **73**
      11./JG 3 (*Sturmstaffel* 1) **57**, 64, 65, 66, 74
      12.(*Sturm*)/JG 3 64, 70, **73**, 75
      13.(*Sturm*)/JG 3 **58**, 76, 78, **79**, 80, 84
      14.(*Sturm*)/JG 3 (*Sturmstaffel* 1) **58**, **75**, 76, **77**, 78, 81, 83, 84
      16.(*Sturm*)/JG 3 71, **73**, 75, 76, 77, 78–79, **82**
    Stab JG 3 6, 7, 8, 11–12, 15, 18, 24, **29**, 31, 33, 37, 38, 40–41, 45, 49, 60, 66, 70–71, 82
  JG 5 80
  JG 7 84
  JG 26 23, 80
    Stab JG 26 8, 9
  JG 27 61, **64**
    8./JG 27 48
    Stab JG 27 7
  JG 51 **69**, 83, 84
    2./JG 51 75
  JG 52 49, 70
    I./JG 52 19
  JG 53 4, 40, 67
    8./JG 53 4
  JG 54 48
  JG 77 30
    II./JG 77 30
    III./JG 77 31
    Stab JG 77 7, 9
  JG 137
    I./JG 137 (I./JG 232) 6
    I./ZG 76 (destroyer wing) 21
    II./JG 137 6, 7
    IV./JG 27 61
  JG 231
    I./JG 231 (I./ZG 2) 6
    II./JG 231 (I./JG 3) 6
    Stab JG 231 6
  Platzschutzstaffel 45–47, **46**
Lüth, Feldwebel Detlev 25, 28
Lützow, Oberstleutnant Günther 4, 7, **7**, 10, 11, **11**, 12, **12**, 15, **17**, 22, 24, **24**, 26, 30, 38, **39**, 40

Massmann, Unteroffizier Matthias 8, 18
Maximowitz, Feldwebel Willi 83–84, **84**
Meckel, Oberleutnant Helmut 17, 20, **21**, **25**, 28
Mediterranean reassignment 32–36, **33**, **36**
Mertens, Hauptmann Helmut **27**, **41**, 60, 71
Michalek, Hauptmann Georg 31, 38, 39
'Mighty Eighth,' the 62
Mölders, Werner 30, 31, 32
Moritz, Major Wilhelm **72**, 72–73, 74–75, 76
Müller, Leutnant Siegfried 79, 81, **82**, 84
Müller, Major Friedrich-Karl 67, **67**
Münster, Feldwebel Leopold 'Poldi' 27, 34, 41, 44, 47, 48, 67, **67**

NCOs 43, 46, **50**, 83
Normandy campaign, the 68–71

Oak Leaves distinction 25, 26, 31, **31**, 34, 40, 41, 43, 47, **50**, 61, 67, 70
Oesau, Hauptmann Walter 19, **19**, 20, 21, **22**, 25, 26
offensive into France **9**, 9–11
Ohlrogge, Feldwebel Walter 14, 31, **34**, 43–44, **44**
Olejnik, Oberltleutnant Robert 23, **23**, 24, 25, **25**, 26

Operations (German)
  Barbarossa (June–December 1941) **22**, 22–30, **23**, **24**, **25**, **26**, **27**, **28**, **29**, 32
  Bodenplatte (January 1945) 80–81
  Paula (June 1940) 11, **11**
  Taifun (October 1941) 30
  Zitadelle (July 1943) 49
overclaiming of kills 13–14, 22–23

Pankalla, Unteroffizier Gerhard 62
Paulus, *Generalfeldmarschall* Friedrich 47
'Phoney War' *(Sitzkrieg)* 7–8
purge of older *Kommodores* 15

Quaet-Faslem, Major Klaus 60, 64, **65**, 70

RAF 'Circus' raids 20
reconnaisance flights 24
Red Air Force, the 36, 48, 83
Red Army resistance 32–33, 36–38, 42–43, 44–45, 46, 47–48, 49, 50
Rentsch, Feldwebel Wolfgang **64**
Rohwer, Hauptmann Detlev **29**, 66
Romm, Oberleutnant Oskar **73**, 75, **82**, 83
Rüffler, Oberfeldwebel Helmut 23, 44, 47, 68–69, **69**
Ruhl, Leutnant Franz 48, **60**, 61, 76, 78

Saborowski, Oberfeldwebel Rudolf 18, 42
Sannemann, Oberleutnant Heinrich 19, 31
Schentke, Oberfeldwebel Georg **42**, 43, 45, **46**, 46–47
Schleef, Leutnant Hans 37, 49, 50, 59, 60, 66
Schnabel, Leutnant Heinz 16, 17–18, **18**
Schroer, Major Werner 82
Schwaiger, Leutnant Franz **36**, 44, 62, 66, **66**
Selle, Hauptmann Erich von 7, 19
Sochatzy, Oberleutnant Kurt 28, **28**
Sperrle, *Generalfeldmarschall* Hugo **71**
Sprenger, Leutnant Gerhard **10**, 11, 19, 21
Staffeln, increase of 70
Stalingrad, Battle of 45, 46–47, 50
Stange, Oberleutnant Willy 14, 23
Stechmann, Feldwebel Hans **18**, **19–20**, 20, **27**, 28
Stukageschwader 2 'Immelmann' 6
Sturmgruppe 66–67
Surau, Oberfeldwebel Alfred 60, **62**, 63
Swords, military distinction 31, 47, **47**, 65, **82**

Tichy, Oberleutnant Ekkehard **74**, 76
Tiedmann, Oberleutnant Helmut 12, 14, **14**
training 72, 74
Troha, Oberleutnant Egon 18–19, **19**
tyros 41, 62, 64, 76

Udet, Generaloberst Ernst **6**, 32
Unger, Leutnant Willi **82**, 84

Vieck, Oberstleutnant Carl 7, 8, 11, 15
Vivroux, Feldwebel Gerhard **75**, 76
Volkmann, Oberleutnant Wilhem-Erich 76

Wald, Feldwebel Harry 71, 78–79, 81, 83
Wallrath, Unteroffizier Karl-Heinz 30, 36–37
Wappler, Oberleutnant Harry 17–18
Werra, Leutnant Franz von 16, **16**, 17–18
Wessling, Oberfeldwebel Otto 20, 38, 39, 63–64, 66, 70
Wielebinski, Feldwebel Paul 62, 69
Wilcke, *Kommodore* Wolf-Dietrich **39**, 40, 47, **47**, **65**, 66
Woitke, Oberleutnant Erich 17, 19

Zimmermann, Leutnant Oskar 78, 81
Zink, Leutnant Dieter 67–70